89619157

I.D 10594507701 me 05/22
02 hash 441

I.D 10594507 01 me
02 David

2522310703

DEMOCRACY AS WE LIVED IT

1922-2005

§

Compiled By

Eugene Tucker

CONTRIBUTING WRITERS
Harriet Burgess
Helen P. Hannett
Keith Severin
Eugene Tucker
Thelma Webb Wright

§

Copyright©2005 by First Library Writing Group
All rights reserved.
(Copyright reverts to individual writers and authors upon publication)
ISBN 0-9623650-2-5
Library of Congress Control Number: 2005903942

Table of Contents

	Page
Dedication	iii
Acknowledgment	v
Foreword	vii
Preface	ix
Introduction	xi

Chapter 1 Those Were The Days — 1
Harriet Burgess	*The Confederate Doctor*	3
Eugene Tucker	*My Old Hussy*	7
Helen P. Hannett	*From the Ukraine to the United States*	15
Thelma Webb Wright	*Those Poor Buggars*	17

Chapter 2 All In The Family — 21
Keith Severin	*From Texas to California*	23
Eugene Tucker	*A Boy of Four*	25
Harriet Burgess	*O'l Tom Gets Stuffed*	27

Chapter 3 Depression Anyone — 29
Eugene Tucker	*Flight North*	31
Harriet Burgess	*Amazing Struggle*	33
Thelma Webb Wright	*I was as Red as the Coat*	39

Chapter 4 At Work And Play — 41
Eugene Tucker	*The Way Things Were*	43
Harriet Burgess	*A 1960's Working Girl*	45
Helen P. Hannett	*The Blizzard of 1996*	49

Chapter 5 Coming of Age — 53
Harriet Burgess	*Life Wasn't Always a 'Bed of Roses'!*	55
Eugene Tucker	*Now What?*	57
Helen P. Hannett	*The Holy Father is Passing by*	61

Chapter 6 Education — 65
Harriet Burgess	*A Simpler Time and a Simpler Place*	67
Thelma Webb Wright	*Education, a Priority?*	71
Eugene Tucker	*Education and Freedom*	75

Chapter 7 The 50's and 60's — 77
Eugene Tucker	*The Struggle*	79
Keith Severin	*A Sleeper*	83
Helen P. Hannett	*I Never Got My Muscles Back*	87
Thelma Webb Wright	*Surviving*	91
Harriet Burgess	*The End of Camelot*	95

(continued) Page

Chapter 8 Wars, Politics, Society — 97

Eugene Tucker	*Therefore Stand*	99
Eugene Tucker	*The Politics of Race*	103
Harriet Burgess	*The Big Put Down*	107
Keith Severin	*Letters To Frank*	109

Chapter 9 Relationships — 117

Harriet Burgess	*Was There a Color Barrier?*	119
Eugene Tucker	*Yes'um*	121
Thelma Webb Wright	*Togetherness*	125
Eugene Tucker	*Who Wears the Pants?*	129
Keith Severin	*It's A Son!*	131

Chapter 10 Those Lasting Impressions — 133

Thelma Webb Wright	*I Hurted So Bad I No Could Cry*	135
Harriet Burgess	*Stories from the Past*	137
Eugene Tucker	*Etched in Memory*	141
Eugene Tucker	*LAW, For Whom?*	145
Helen P. Hannett	*Remembering Dad*	147
Keith Severin	*Spring Is On The Way*	151

Chapter 11 Life Shaping Events — 153

Helen P. Hannett	*Eisenhower, Daddy and Me*	155
Eugene Tucker	*Events that Shaped My Life*	159
Eugene Tucker	*A Test of Faith*	163

Chapter 12 Reflections — 169

Thelma Webb Wright	*To my Granddaughter, Katherine*	171
Keith Severin	*Development! Development!*	173
Harriet Burgess	*The Old Iron Kettle*	175
Harriet Burgess	*World War II Reflections*	177
Eugene Tucker	*My Dad*	181
Helen P. Hannett	*My Love of Books*	185

Chapter 13 Words of Wisdom — 191

Eugene Tucker	*Now Hear This*	193

Biographical Sketches — 197

Dedicated to

Eugene Tucker

Who suggested at our last class meeting, we should and could compile a book of our experiences in the 20th century.
We agreed we "should" but the "could" only became possible with Gene's guidance, his endless hours of editing, organizing and
expert computer talent.
Gene, we thank you for the three years you devoted to this project.

ACKNOWLEDGEMENT

This book would not have been possible without the confidence and support of Ms. Dawn Sowers of the Fauquier County Public Library, who accepted a proposal from Thelma Webb Wright to offer a short memories writing course for senior citizens designed to last only a few months in the fall of 2002. The official class ended as winter approached and our wonderful instructor, Thelma, headed for warmer climates in Florida. The class continued when the idea was presented to develop a joint book. For over two years Dawn provided a room in the children's section of the library and supplied us with tea and coffee on the first Monday of each month and always greeted us with a warm smile. Of the original group of ten, four remained and was joined by Thelma upon her return to Virginia the following spring. Thelma deserves special mention for her support and determination that we complete this "worthwhile" project. Her imprint is on every page in this book including her own written contributions. This book may never have been completed were it not for her dedication to the effort and constant encouragement.

Finally, I want to thank and congratulate each member of the group for accepting my idea for the book and trusting me to guide its completion. I am humbled by the unimagined work ethic, warmth and support you gave me.

Eugene Tucker

FOREWORD

For three years a group of senior American citizens met each month in the children's room of a small country library in Fauquier County, Virginia. The expectation was that a short course on writing our memories would not be too invasive and that we might get better insights on how best to document some of our thoughts and recollections developed over the years. The exercise seemed harmless enough, so most of the participants continued to come to the sessions each month and read our carefully crafted two or three page vignettes to the class. Our charming and demanding instructor, herself an accomplished writer, laid out the ground rules and offered suggestions on how to select topics, structure them, and most importantly preserve them. Honesty in our writings was the hallmark demanded by the instructor. This would be a challenge, for some of us thought this would bring back some unpleasant memories, open old wounds, and rattle the bones of skeletons long since locked away in our closets and in our minds. I first attended the class out of curiosity and thought this might give me incentive to continue work on some old manuscripts I had begun over forty years ago. A little prodding would do me some good. I have always been a loner and I never thought that a short course in writing would do more than, perhaps, give me momentum. This narrow vision soon began to change as I listened attentively as each person revealed a little portion of themselves. It became apparent that this course had taken on a new and deeper meaning for all of us. Each of us looked forward to each class session and apologized when we were not prepared or could not attend. Yet, attendance seemed more important than the preparation. If there were trepidation about what to reveal at the beginning, one could easily notice the lowering of defenses with each class encounter. I noticed the impact these encounters was having on each of us. It was cathartic. It was "OK" to be honest.

I began to reflect on the term "We the people..." as I sat there with ordinary people like me. It occurred to me that we were having a dialogue about freedom and democracy not written in our text books or discussed in public discourse. The United States Constitution begins this way

> *We the people of the United States, in Order to form a more perfect Union, establish Justice, insure domestic Tranquility, provide for the common defense, promote the general Welfare, and secure the Blessings of Liberty to ourselves and our Posterity, do ordain and establish this Constitution for the United States of America.*

Sitting around the table and enjoying the stories from people whose origins began in countries like Russia, Germany, Poland, Ireland, and the native settlers in this land, I pondered those words from our "Founding Fathers".

Some of the people sharing a table with me were here because America represented a new beginning for their forefathers. Some arrive to escape oppression in their native country. Still others sought adventure and fortune. While some had been greeted by Lady Liberty, my ancestors had arrived chained in the bowels of slave ships. Yet, here we are seated together revealing a life and time we all share. Our little stories revealed a common thread. We brought something to the table that our "Founding Fathers" could not have imagined when they crafted the Constitution. Most of us know of the existence of the Constitution; few have read it completely, while even fewer have ever tried to interpret it. This is true for most of the enacted laws that govern our country and affect each and every one of us daily.

When that most important document was written, I was considered only 3/5 of a man and was being held as chattel. However, there were some revealing statements in this document that ultimately laid the foundation for "democracy". The phrase "...more perfect Union,..." recognized that more work was needed in order to "establish Justice" and "insure domestic Tranquility". I was challenged to take a fresh look at the Constitution while sitting at the table each month and listening to the revealing stories. A great war had been fought for our Liberty. Another great war had been fought among ourselves to give freedom to the slaves. It would take a century to implement a law that freed the slave. Again in our history there was more bloodshed triggered by a massive social upheaval in the 1960's. I finally realized while sitting at this table here in a country library in Fauquier County that each of our families, whether they came willingly from foreign lands or whether they arrived by slave ship, has unknowingly contributed to the definition of democracy. Democracy is a fluid and dynamic concept. Each generation defines and interprets its meaning, sometimes overlapping with those established by past generations, but never without conflict. Laws are written as guidelines. People and their families interpret and implement them within their own personal framework and circumstance. As we have seen over the generations the interpretations and implementations often conflict with law, many resulting with a date at the Supreme Court. Our generation continues to define democracy that is why I am now able to sit at the table. This book, written by a group of people who could not have sat together or separately at the same table in the United States when our lives began, is a testament that democracy has evolved and Liberty has been defined.

Eugene Tucker

Preface

The stories you are about to read are ethnographies presented by a group of citizens residing in Fauquier County Virginia at the beginning of the 21st century. Their lives began in the 20th century with family ties to the 19th century and links to many cultures throughout the world. They are in a unique position to reflect on the past, record their journey through the 20th century, and anticipate what may lie ahead in the 21st century. One may say that they have a world view as an "ordinary man", steeped in experience in having been there through the years. They have seen evolution and revolution and have taken part in both, sometimes knowingly and sometimes unknowingly. They witnessed the rise and fall of governments in various parts of our world. They witnessed the rise and fall of many prominent leaders throughout our world. They witnessed famine here in our country and around the world. They witnessed the expansion of our nation with the annexation of Alaska and Hawaii. They witnessed the changing of our socio-economic cultures; struggles between the races; corporate greed; challenges to religion; the expansion of the human intellect and the challenge to morality. They have witnessed and participated in the ever evolving struggle to define "Democracy".

Indeed they know from whence they come, where they have been, and have a notion of where we are headed. Recorded on these pages are the accounts of a diverse people whose stories will provide a glimpse of a life and time in American history that are told by those who lived it and not by anthropologists who can only speculate from artifacts left from a distant past. This is a story of a journey through life told by people not known to each other before the writing of this book. None, perhaps, are known as world leaders, yet each in his or her own way individually and collectively continues to contribute to the universal experience called life.

Several questions are addressed. Can a group of people from different backgrounds, with different experiences, from different ethnic backgrounds, and with different world views collaborate to write a book? Are there topics too sensitive to allow honest dialogue? Are there events in our lives that must remain secret even to the grave? Is there any value to such a book? Who would read it? The effort in putting this book together has answered these questions for the writers. Now it's your turn to see if we succeeded.

INTRODUCTION

In October of year 2002, a group of citizens responded to an advertisement sponsored by the Fauquier County Public Library. The library offered a writing course on preserving memories. Some ten people responded on the first day, but increased in number as the weeks passed. At first there were two men who attended on a regular basis. Several other men would attend later, but only briefly. Our teacher and mentor was a charming woman who was a successful author. She was well organized and offered many very insightful suggestions, while motivating each of us in ways most of us had not been motivated since our early years in school. Preservation became the operative word during each session. Print on paper had to be preserved. Acid free paper and jackets for our writings and photographs were demanded from each of us with bits and pieces of paper archived and dated. We were here because we had planned or were working on manuscripts, albums, documentaries, or some method to communicate what we thought important markers to leave to our children, grandchildren, and a history of our families for generations to follow us. We all had something to say and time was of the essence, since many of our lives began during the 1930's and before. We were carrying around memories of our journey through life in our heads, in photographs and in our hearts. Boxes of files had been stored in attics, under beds, in storage sheds, and scattered among family members around the country and indeed around the world. Someone was needed to organize and preserve all of this family history before the links to the past and to our mother land would be lost forever. We were that someone. So, here we were a tiny cluster of people representing the American experience in Fauquier County Virginia, USA.

As each class session unfolded with our vignettes being read aloud for all to hear, similarities and differences soon became apparent. One member contrasted his upbringing to John Steinbeck's *The Grapes of Wrath*. A famous line uttered by the heroine from that prize winning book was recalled. *"We're the people, you can't kill us out. We just keep on coming!"* Others did not experience the sting of the 1930's depression, while others had only a passing knowledge of the horrors of segregation. Each shared story opened a tiny window into the lives of this diverse group of people. There were guarded stories too painful to share, and hidden secrets now opened for all to hear, and once thought truths were now open to question. The process of discovery was being pursued by each of us. We were beginning to see ourselves as we never saw ourselves before and to understand the many forces and circumstances that have shaped our lives. For some there was a trail to follow though slow and painful. For others verification of many of the stories would not be possible. Only the utterances of the village storyteller and oral histories would provide the clues to the past. How do we write this stuff? And, who wants to know? Who will read it? These were some of the questions on our minds as each vignette left our pens.

Chapter 1

THOSE WERE THE DAYS

A little house well fill'd, a little land well till'd,
a little wife well will'd, are great riches
                               John Ray, English Proverbs

THE CONFEDERATE DOCTOR
Harriet Burgess

My maternal great-grandfather was Dr. William David McWhorter. His ancestry was Scotch-Irish, tracing his roots in America to before the Revolution. His father was the Rev. William McWhorter, a Presbyterian of Calvinistic background with a love of the classics. His mother, Margaret Kyle McWhorter, wanted her first child to be born at her home in Pontotoc County, Mississippi.

William David was born on December 27, 1838, the eldest of five children. Shortly afterwards the family returned to the McWhorter home, 'Bachelor's Retreat' in Pickens, South Carolina. Here in a home which is still standing, William David grew up.

Becoming interested in medicine, he attended the Medical College of South Carolina and received his doctor of medicine degree in 1860, signed by Jefferson Davis. With the outbreak of the Civil War, Dr. McWhorter offered his services to the Confederacy and served on the medical staff of Col. James L. Orr's Regiment, known as 'Orr's Rifles.'

The fortunes of war led him to Fairfax County, where he met his future bride, Miss Mary Jones Millan of The Hermitage, near Chantilly. They met in the aftermath of the Battle of Chantilly (Ox Hill) which occurred September 1, 1862, and was the one large battle fought in Fairfax County during the war. Both The Hermitage and neighboring Avon were turned into improvised hospitals. At Avon, Dr. McWhorter was the surgeon in charge and Mary Jones Millan was one of the volunteer nurses. Miss Millan also became friendly with Col. John S. Mosby and during the war she both sang and played the piano for the famous Confederate raider.

A Civil War story involving Dr. McWhorter's practice in Fairfax County has survived. In a minor skirmish at Gooding's Tavern on the Little River Turnpike (near present day Pickett Shopping Center), a Confederate soldier, John Ballard, was severely wounded in the leg. Dr. McWhorter was called to attend to him. Deciding he would have to sacrifice the limb to save his life, Dr. McWhorter called on the services of a passerby to help with the improvised operation. The passerby happened to be Alexander Haight of Sully Plantation, and his grandson recalled the story as it was passed down to him. They stretched Ballard on the table and the doctor clapped a handful of wood ashes onto the side of his head. He told Alexander where to hit him with a stick of firewood which knocked him cold. The ashes supposedly softened the blow a bit. Somehow the operation was successful. The patient not only recovered but married the girl at whose home the operation was performed. Ballard was later to become Fairfax County Commissioner of Revenue.

Following the war, Dr. McWhorter returned to his home in South Carolina, but waged another Fairfax campaign. This one was by mail in an effort to win the hand of the attractive Miss Mary Millan. (Theirs was a celebrated love affair, and their letters during the latter part of the Civil War have been preserved.) Family tradition says that William David and his younger brother, James Kyle, were campaigning in Fairfax County during the war and spotted two pretty girls seated on a swing on the front porch of The Hermitage, their pug noses showing coyly beneath their bonnets. The brothers vowed to return after the war to marry them. They did.

Many of the letters of William David and Mary Millan have survived. They reveal a well-educated, determined man, bold in his professions of love to a girl he actually knew only slightly. In making his suit he wrote, *"Therefore I will tell you truthfully something of myself. I am not wealthy, Miss Mary, and all our negroes (of which there were many) have been taken from us so we are reduced in property, but I am comfortably situated yet. And it would be my earnest desire to make you comfortable and happy."* Later he agreed with Mary's observation that contentment is better than wealth but added he would not object to a little wealth along with contentment.

His year long suit was successful and the wedding took place at The Hermitage in Fairfax County on November 27, 1866. The couple in time had seven children, one of which was my grandfather, Pinckney Lee.

William David McWhorter, MD (1838-1895)
First President of Fairfax Medical Society

Mary Jones Lee (Millan) McWhorter (1844-1895)
Wearing her Civil War Nursing Uniform

Dr. McWhorter's brother, James who was also a Civil War veteran, became a physician and fell in love with and married Mary's younger sister, Virginia. Following his marriage to Mary, Dr. David McWhorter made Fairfax County his home and in time joined the Marr Camp of Confederate Veterans. His letters to his family in South Carolina give an insight into his medical practice and also tell about conditions in Fairfax following the war. In 1868, Dr. McWhorter proudly wrote his father and brother about his growing practice.

"Have had as much practice as could possibly attend to for some time. Have done $60 of good for the week ending today and have not lost any yet by death. Some days get as many as three calls to new cases yet the country is not sickly. Darkeys are cash paying here and can pay from 8 to 20 dollars as easy as many whites in Pickens."

It is clear that McWhorter had numerous patients and, despite his background as a South Carolina slave holder, he did not generally use denigrating language in discussing the blacks. He ended his letter by indicating *"I may buy a lot in the town of Fairfax, but like home-buyers before and after the war, I will have to pay more than originally expected. The cost ended up being $2,000 but the home had 'seven rooms and a fine basement dining room besides all other out-buildings."*

In another letter he referred to *"drawing off nearly 5 gallons of water from an old lady who has the dropsy. Have had almost more obstetric cases lately than anything else."* The life of a country doctor was not easy, and Dr. McWhorter had some serious misgivings about his arduous life. In 1871 he wrote, *"Myself and horse are pretty stiff. Some days I ride about 50 miles. Have had but few nights rest together this summer."* At that period of time taxes were very high and money was slow to come in. He writes, *"Have never been able to collect more at a time than was needed for family expenses."* Discouraged, he confessed, *"Wish I had an easier way of making a living sometimes, but don't believe I am fit for anything else.."* In 1872 he complained, *"Have had more sickness than I could attend well for some time and not a dollar coming in cash."* At this time he mentions losing patients, *"a lady of 77 years old of typhoid fever and a negro man 61 of dropsy."*

Later the same year he wrote,

"I dread another winter's practice for last winter I was so crippled up from the cold as to be almost unfit for duty and I think I will have to give up practice entirely if I remain here much longer, though this is a fine healthy climate and we are tolerably comfortably situated."
"Help is very hard to get with servants, both black and white, being unreliable. Servants are the plague of the house keeper now. Takes all the money to pay them for staying with you and doing almost nothing."

To help alleviate the problem, he planned to go to the Orphan Asylum in Washington to get a 10-year-old girl. *"She will be bound to us until she is 18 years old."* In 1873 he wrote *"I do not know of any one yet to whom I might sell out so we could go to southern Virginia."* He desires to move although he 'still has plenty of practice.' In 1874 his beloved wife came down with typhoid fever which caused new hardships for the doctor. *"I wish I was in a farm and all well. Have several possibilities for selling."* Having to take care of Mary, he was forced to give up his practice. He writes, *"Practice would be heavy if I could attend to it. Have calls every day."*

The winters definitely were harsher in the early days than they are now. In the winter of 1876-77 he did not see the ground between the end of November and the end of January. The weather did markedly affect his travel, *"Have only gone out about once or twice a week to see special cases and never go out at night."* It was hard on his health as he suffered from rheumatism. He lamented. *"If I could only sell out here for near the worth of my property, I would not be exposed through compulsion. I cannot stand any exposure now without being made sick."*

In May of 1884 he was elected President of the Fairfax County Medical Society. In County Court Minutes Books Dr. McWhorter is noted as being paid $5 twice for examining men charged with lunacy. In 1891 he was paid $10 for conducting an inquest.

Early in the 1890s the McWhorters moved to Washington, D.C. and lived on 11th Street North East. Dr. McWhorter practiced in Washington until his death in 1895 when he was taken with pneumonia. His final years are shrouded in mystery and the family was reduced to severe financial stress, caused by poor health and uncollected medical bills. After the Civil War, very few families could afford the services of a physician and would pay him in chickens and feed or not pay at all. The family had to pawn a good deal of their jewelry and furniture to meet expenses.

Dr. McWhorter's health was failing for some time, and his beloved wife became terminally ill, apparently suffering from cancer. Against this sad background he died on February 20, 1895, at Providence Hospital in Washington, DC at the age of 56. Only two weeks later his wife also passed away at Columbia Hospital at the age of 50. They are both buried at the Old Congressional Cemetery in Washington, D.C.

Dr. William David McWhorter was a man of considerable ability and well respected by his peers. Little could he realize that the Medical Society over which he first presided in 1884 with 13 members would grow to over 70 members, and by financing a history of the Medical Society saved his name from virtual obscurity in the history of Fairfax County Virginia.

MY OLD HUSSY
Eugene Tucker

For nine months Mom nurtured me in the safety of her womb. About 2am on the morning of January 13, in the year 1935, it was finally time for me to meet my mother face to face. The knee deep snow, rare for this part of the south, made it impossible for Mom to reach the little hospital some four miles away. So, Aunt Ellen, the often called upon midwife, was summoned to deliver Mom's third child. Aunt Ellen lived in the third house up the hill on this country clay dirt road about a half mile away. She looked at least twice her size from all the layers of clothes she wore. Her head was wrapped with a red Pullman's handkerchief. I remember her as being quite a feisty woman about five feet seven inches tall. It was not safe to travel these woods in the dark. Bears, panthers, fox, and other nocturnal creatures roamed these woods in search of prey. There were accounts of humans being attacked by predators during the night. There were no lights, sidewalks, or travelers. Only the bright sky and moon made travel safe in this desolate place. We were just "cross Bogue" in the Mississippi woods a few miles from Tie Plant, Mississippi.

Aunt Ellen's home site, only the chimney remains

Aunt Ellen was quite efficient since she had performed this function many times before. From accounts of this event from my older sisters, Uncle Charlie, and Dad, Aunt Ellen came into our two room shanty and started ordering people around. The room was lit by kerosene lamps and Mom lay in bed in the back room close to the wood stove. This was our kitchen. Water was put on the stove to boil as Aunt Ellen gathered rags and towels and prepared for the delivery. My oldest sister, Eunice, was ordered to hold the lamp. Aunt Ellen spoke in a harsh voice,

"Chap, hold this lamp so you can see! May be you won't go mess yo'self up!"

"Y'all git out de way!"

The delivery was easy and Mom and I saw each other for the first time. I can not imagine what went through her mind when she first laid eyes on her son. I would be her only son; Leona would come thirteen months later. As Mom looked upon her baby child and as I gazed about the darken room neither one of us could anticipate what was ahead. What an amazing journey this would be for two souls joined together by birth on this early morning in the Mississippi woods and touched by the hand of fate. From all accounts I must have weighed approximately seven pounds with shiny black hair to match my soft dark skin. I shed few tears as I surveyed this place of my birth.

This is my place of birth; behind these bushes and trees was the house where I was born.

Our relationship and my journey would start here in this little shanty in the woods. I would not be breast fed, since Mom's milk had been dried up after the birth of my sister Lorene. Mom had been instructed to use alum and some other herb to dry up her milk from her last pregnancy some five years earlier. So, Mom used "pot liquor", the juice from greens placed in a gauze sack made to resemble a nipple, and cow's milk to feed me. When I became old enough to eat table food, Mom would mash some cornbread with the pot liquor and feed me with a spoon. I soon learned to suck my thumb which continued until I was almost ten years old. Mom tried everything to keep me from sucking my thumb: black pepper, quinine, garlic, iodine, and any other distasteful substance she could find to place or wrap on my thumb. Yet, the sucking persisted, especially at night while I was sleeping. She would often sneak up behind me and yank my thumb from my mouth. I became more conscious of the habit and stopped several years later after we moved to Louisville, Kentucky in the 1940's.

As a child I had ear aches, sore throat, and a regular case of hives. A dose of black drough, castor oil, Epson salt, or sassafras teas was quickly available for my ailments. Then there was sweet gum and a match stick used for cleaning teeth. Dad used something called jimson weed to treat his asthma. I don't remember much about our little shanty in the woods. I was told about the hardship and struggle to survive.

My family moved to the city of Grenada about six miles away when I was about two years old. Our house was a little shanty on Railroad Avenue about the same size and style as the one I was born in. I have clear memories of the dusty road covered with gravel that I played in with bare feet and the string around my neck which carried a small ball of some stinky substance to help with my occasional nose bleed. I played hide and seek under the house that was supported by six brick support pillars. Leona would play with me when she was able to walk and chase after me. Mom swept the yard around the house every morning and checked for the occasional snake that found its way near the house. She kept a hoe by the rear door just in case it was needed. Dad was working at Tie Plant and Mom took in washing and ironing to help support the family. By the time I was five years old Eunice had gotten pregnant and Mom had sent her from our house. I remember Mom humming a tune early one morning as she gathered Eunice's belongings and placed them in a sack at the front door. I heard Mom say,

> "You're a woman now. There is only room for one woman in this house, so you must leave. I can't have my baby children seeing this!"

Eunice would never live with Mom again. Eunice married Sam Black, a fair skin man from Holcolm, Mississippi and moved into a little shanty a few houses from us on Railroad Avenue. My second oldest sister, Lorene, remained with our family. We moved to Louisville, Kentucky and Eunice followed a short time later with her baby son. By now I was beginning to question any and everything I heard and saw. Mom became the focal point of my inquiry. I followed her around watching her every move. Before long I began to understand that our relationship was becoming strained as I continued to challenge and raise questions, many of which she had no ready answers. For me there was nothing off limits.

"You didn't follow the recipe."

"You're not doing that right!"

"That's not the way you did it the last time."

"I know how to make the draperies, let me do it."

"I'll show you how to crochet the pocket in that sweater."

To Mom's chagrin I was often right, but she would not admit it to me, so I continued. Soon, Dad would sense the tension and would take me to work with him as often as he could. They figured out the best way to handle me was to keep me busy--cleaning the floors, washing windows, landscaping, building things around the house, chopping wood, even grocery shopping. I enjoyed every task and asked for more. They discovered I had taught myself to read, so books would be given to me so I could search for answers to my questions about the universe, human anatomy, airplanes, how things work. They had given me the world and I could hardly wait harassing Mom to explore it. School was too boring so I did not participate. I just wanted to go home to work on my projects, which consisted of making things from wood and harassing mom. My grade school teachers determined I was retarded and held me back in second grade. Now, Leona and I were in the same grade. This did not alter my attitude about school. She excelled. I lagged behind as the teachers passed me along with my sister. Things would change when we reached fifth grade. Our teacher discovered that I could do geometry and algebra. My sister and I were tested and sent to junior high school. My attitude towards school did not change much here until my mother offered me a bribe to bring home grades as good as my sister's. I decided to seek the money and the next grading period I brought home strait A's like my sister. To my surprise no money changed hands. I had been exposed and now threatened if I showed lack of effort again. I knew these were no idle threats coming from my mother.

As the years passed and I became an adult, Mom and I would continue our tug of war. When I left home and the city to start a life on my own, Mom wept. I would phone her almost daily and we would talk. When she picked up the phone she would hear

"What are you doing, Old Woman?", or

"How's my old hussy today?"

This would usually spark some heated dialogue, which later turned friendly once she got use to my antics. When I came home to visit, I was greeted as her prince.

However, the next morning we would have our regular argument over anything or nothing, resulting in her crying and me hugging her and telling her that I loved her. These events would take place throughout our lives together no matter where we were. I didn't think she loved me and she thought I did not love her. So we continued to harass each other, but we could not stand to be without each other.

    A few years after I had left home Dad became ill with a blood clot on the brain. Medical science at that time was not advanced enough to attempt the removal of the clot without severe risk. So, Dad had to retire from his job before he was sixty years old. Mom and Dad asked me to come home and meet with their lawyer. They decided to have a life estate formed and transferred their property to me. For a short while my oldest sister was not satisfied with their decision. She thought the oldest child should control their affairs. My parents would have a home for the remainder of their lives and I would be responsible for maintaining the property. My parents felt completely secure with their decision. For more than five years we watched a once vibrant man deteriorate and lose control of his life. Mom became his full time nurse. The toll on her was increasingly difficult. My sisters who had remained in the city pitched in to help. I phoned every day and almost every weekend I boarded an airplane and went home to relieve my mother for two days. I remembered the days when I would sit on his lap and brush his hair until he went to sleep; the days he trusted me to install tile on the walls of our first in-house bathroom; the day he brought home a set of blueprints for an airport runway; the day he showed up with a set of books that had been sanctioned by the US Congress on the writings of the Presidents; and all those parts he brought me to build a radio and convinced my mother to let me plug it into the electrical outlet. What a moment that was when audible sounds came followed by a large puff of smoke. It was Dad who trusted me to remodel our kitchen over my Mother's strong objections, removing interior and exterior doors and windows, moving plumbing and electrical wires and building and installing cabinets. I was still in high school at the time. Dad made me draw a set of plans and submit them to the city for approval and supervised the work. To Mom's surprise I successfully accomplished the task during summer break from school. For years Mom would talk to anyone who would listen about her new kitchen. Even the color of the paint has not been changed. Dad would die before his sixty fifth birthday.

    Mom would remain in the house alone. When I went home now, I would always ring the doorbell and wait for her to answer and let me in. I did not think it was wise to use my key to enter the house. Mom was quite a skilled marksman.

    Mom became my princess. Garfinckel was an upscale department store in Washington, DC that caught my eye. It had the Greenbrier Room where men could sit and have models show off women's fashions. There was a model with the same measurements as my mother. I would go there and have dresses, suits, coats, and accessories modeled before me. I would make selections and have them sent home to Mom. At first Mom protested that I was spending too much. After a while the complaints stopped as she would proudly wear them when I came home. We would visit our relatives and stay out late into the night. On one of our night visits with Mom's brother, Uncle Charlie, I was amazed to witness how much they enjoyed each other. They played music, danced, told stories and laughed until after 2am.

I remembered Mom telling me not to answer the door when our cousin, Leslie Whitfield, came to visit. Mom said

"That old fool will come here and stay all day!"

He would knock for a long time and then walk away mumbling to himself. We would visit his house and would have a hard time leaving as he escorted us to the car and continued talking while we drove away. I wanted to listen to him talk about the bible, growing up in the country, his brothers and sisters even if we had to spend the night. He talked loud and laughed hardily showing his mouth full of gold. He was quite an entrepreneur. He obtained a license to lend money and made loans to people on his job. His house was full of items he had taken as collateral. He waited for his clients every payday to collect. He said to me as he sat back in his chair and grinned.

"Boy, see this house! I paid cash for it and that car sitting out there."

He would express his dissatisfaction whenever I came home and did not come to visit him. So, I would make every effort to visit him and all of my relatives and many of their friends to lessen the complaints directed to Mom.

One day I asked Mom to visit me in California. She was quite reluctant to answer. She was afraid to fly, since she had never been on an airplane before. Leona offered to give her a trial run by asking Mom to join her on trip to New York by air. Mom trusted Leona with her life and accepted the trip. They visited New York and stopped over in Washington, DC. To my surprise Mom was not frightened and enjoyed the flight. Now, she had an answer to the California offer. This time my sister, Lorene, would accompany Mom on the long flight from Louisville, Kentucky to Los Angeles, California. I met them at the airport and retrieved their luggage. Mom was radiant with a big grin on her face. We were thrilled to see each other. Mom told me all about the trip as we drove to the hotel. The next morning Mom and I had our usual argument over some unimportant topic I don't remember. She threatened to return to the airport and leave for home. Shortly there after we patched things up, hugged and planned our day. What fun we had in Disney Land and dinner that evening in a Chinese restaurant where Mom tried to use chop sticks. We visited the Universal Studios in Hollywood, where one of the stars from the Monsters tried to pinch her rear. That almost caused a major crisis. How she enjoyed Beverly Hills and seeing all the mansions and stores. She was like a little girl when we walked the beaches of Santa Monica bare foot. This trip would be a defining moment in our relationship. For the first time I realized how intelligent Mom was and how much fun it was to be around her. It had taken me thirty five years to discover Mom.

Mom flanked by daughters Leona (l) and Lorene ® at a wedding ceremony at Lorene's house

We decided to take a trip together the following year to New Orleans, Louisiana.

During the ensuing months Mom and I would talk, argue, and make up as usual. I told Mom about the stock market and she admonished me for gambling. I told her about baseball and other things I enjoyed doing. Mom was full of surprises. One day she asked me about a security I had mentioned to her.

"Have you sold that stock?" she asked.

"Why" I asked.

"You probably should have sold it last week." she replied.

Mom had started to watch the stock market and understood as much as I. I was astounded by this and her announcement that she had sat through all nine innings of Don Larsen's no hit performance in the world series.

Mom enjoyed working around the house and in the yard. After I had a new garage built, Mom decided to paint it. She was quite skilled and painting was a good exercise, she thought. She did not realize how hot it was on this day and suffered a mild heat stroke. She did not think much of it, since she had spent much of her life in the hot sun. However, her condition was more severe than she thought. Medical exams after medical exams did not solve her problem. Her mental capacity had been affected. Then, arthritis began to cripple her hands and knees. There would be no trip for us to

New Orleans. Mom's health slowly deteriorated over the next several years. She became bed ridden and a full time nurse had to be hired to look after her. She had refused to allow my oldest sister, Eunice, to live with her after she was sent from our house when I was a little boy. It was too difficult for my other two sisters to stay overnight with Mom. Eventually, Mom had to be placed in a nursing home. She received daily visits from members of our family.

Our traditional Christmas parties had to be relocated to Lorene's house. By now Mom and Lorene had become Jehovah Witnesses. But this did not stop our family's celebration. I never missed a year from being at home at Christmas. I prepared the menu, the meals, and organized the celebration for all to come. Family members from Chicago, Michigan, Ohio, Tennessee, and Indiana would converge on Lorene's little house. We would not forget to send part of our meal to someone identified as being in need. I could find no greater joy than this and everyone would ask long in advance if Baby Brother, the only name I was known by, is coming home. The matriarch of this gathering could no longer be present, but our prayers were always with her. When I went home for Christmas 1986, I visited Mom in the hospital where she had been recently transferred from the nursing home. This time she did not respond to my conversation. I don't think she recognized me as she labored for each breath with tightly closed eyes. I sat with her rubbing her back and arms for more than an hour. The joy of this Christmas would be muted by the thoughts of Mom. Before my return trip to Washington, DC I stopped by the hospital to see Mom. She appeared to be in the same position which I had left her days earlier. Her breathing was more labored now. As I looked upon her motionless body I remembered the little shanties in Grenada, Mississippi, the sacrifices she made for me, the confrontations we enjoyed, the roles we played in each others lives, and the fun we shared. As I turned to leave the room and recorded the sight of Mom on the hospital bed, I knew it was time to say good-by. Mom died one day after my birthday on January 14, 1986. It has taken me 28 years to cry.

From the Ukraine to the United States
Helen P. Hannett

My paternal grandfather Michal's family were Cossacks from Kiev in the Ukraine. For centuries the brave Cossacks not only kept invaders out of Ukraine and Russia, but they also succeeded in keeping Gengis Khan out of Europe. Cossack families had discipline, skills, ability to get things done, camaraderie, and the ability to save.

Michal, born in 1887, was a leader and the oldest of many brothers. He had no sisters. He was a Russian Orthodox. He was a skilled carpenter and could build anything. He also was a skilled farmer. My paternal grandmother, Aniela, came from Poland. She had many sisters and no brothers. She was Catholic. Vivacious Aniela was skilled at sewing and farming. She was a good teacher. Both Michal and Aniela were fluent in Ukrainian, Polish and English. They surrounded themselves with many books.

Legend has it that my grandpa was betrothed to my grandmother's oldest sister, but he fell in love with my grandmother. As the youngest of many daughters, grandma had to wait for the others to marry before her. Michal had also fallen in love with the idea of the United States of America. *"It is an honor and privilege to pay taxes in America,"* he would say later. They decided to come to America and marry.

In the early 1900's Michal and Aniela made the long journey by boat to the United States with some of their family. Michal was joined by his cousins, one named George, and two younger brothers, Metro and Fred. Aniela was joined by two older sisters. The journey across the Atlantic had to have been hard, but it was made easier by both the love of the family that shared the same heritage on the trip and by the promise of later bringing over to the new country many other family members.

When they arrived in the United States, there was a whirl of weddings in which they all starred or participated. The weddings were beautiful with exquisite hand made dresses and bouquets with all the Ukrainians and Poles in attendance. Grandma and grandpa settled in Boston, Massachusetts and lived near family and cousins in this country. They also associated and did business with earlier Ukrainian and Polish immigrants and relatives from the old country. The photographer who did their wedding pictures must have been from Ukraine or Poland because of the distinctive quality and detail of those portraits.

Near Boston, Massachusetts, all the Ukrainian brothers and male cousins bought houses within two square blocks of each other, intersected by a road. Each block was considered a different township, like Mattapan or Roslindale. They bought houses close to each other, and also bought all the shares in the social hall in the neighborhood. The nearby cemetery is also filled with family names. When Michal and Aniela bought 52 acres of land for a summer place out in South Hanson, my grandmother's Polish sisters and girl cousins also bought land within walking distance of each other there. That became the backdrop for our family story starting in America.

A Family Gathering in the 1930's

THOSE POOR BUGGERS
Thelma Webb Wright

In reflecting back to my beginning I seem to first think of my father, Robert Webb. At the age of 22 he was a camouflage artist for the U.S. Navy during WW I, and stationed in Norfolk, Virginia. He met my mother, who was a Yeomanette, (the first service branch created for women in the Navy). She was also stationed in Norfolk, Virginia. The Yankee sailor from Massachusetts fell in love with the most beautiful girl he had ever seen. Rosa Newbern was a slender southern belle from Elizabeth City, North Carolina with large brown eyes to match her auburn hair. Dad was discharged in 1921 along with other service men because the government ran out of money. He married Rosa and they began their life together in Methuen, Massachusetts where he was born and where his family lived. Rosa had no family.

Their first child, Hannah, delivered by and named after Dad's mother, arrived in April 1921. Two years later I joined the family.

All of the Webb clan decided to migrate to Florida for a new life and warmer weather. They settled in Lake Worth, on the east coast. Dad soon had a job decorating Palm Beach mansions for the famous architect, Addison Mizner. Another well known architect, Dwight James Baum, was designing a mansion on the west coast for John Ringling, the circus owner. Baum traveled to see Dad's work on the east coast, liked it, and borrowed him from Mizner to work on Ringling's home Ca'd'Zan. (House of John in Venetian dialect)

The Webbs moved from the east coast to live in Sarasota on the west coast. I was still in the diaper stage of life, so my memories are not truly mine only hear say from family stories. The one I like best is about Mrs. Ringling giving Hannah and me a doll for Christmas. Hannah's doll had real hair, mine only had an imprint of hair. I took the scissors and cut the hair off Hannah's doll. That clever action may very well have been the seed to why my sister and I never had a close, loving relationship.

My own memories began when we moved from Sarasota, Florida to a 2nd floor apartment in Montclair, New Jersey. Dwight Baum needed Dad to decorate a large church. My paternal grandparents came from Florida to spend the summer in a cooler climate and to help my mother. (Unbeknown at the time, Mother was in the early stage of Parkinson's).

Grandma Webb gave Hannah, her name sake, a beautiful watch for her birthday. Twelve days later she gave me a tiny ring for my birthday. Like cutting the hair off the doll, I reacted. I threw the ring at my grandmother, had a tantrum and ended up receiving a lecture of how Hannah was special because she was the oldest and also named after grandma. My four year old mind didn't accept the reasoning.

During my second grade of education, we moved from Montclair to the small town of Cedar Grove where Dad was in the process of building a house with the "best Goddamn basement in town."

That was an undisputed fact because Dad and his work buddy, Charley, had stopped at an auction in Verona. They had had enough drinks from Turner's Bar to be happy and to join in the fun of bidding on whatever was being auctioned. Dad became the owner of the stone jailhouse that had to be removed from its site within a short given time. To save face, he purchased a lot in Cedar Grove, then stone by stone the jail was hauled to the lot and our house was built!

In the fall of 1931 we moved in amid saw horses, wood chips and no heat. According to Dad we had a roof over our heads, clothes on our body and food to eat. What the hell more could we want in a day?

The first winter was rough. The marble slab floor in the bathroom was cold to bare feet. Hannah and I not only shared the second bedroom on the first floor but we had to share the same bed. We fought each night about who had a foot or arm extending in the other's area. Dad came in one night, pulled the cover off, twisted one blanket into a rope, placed it down the center of the bed and said, *"You each stay on your own side and I don't want to hear another damn word."* Then we fought as to who caused the problem.

At the time, I was never aware that our country was in a severe depression. Looking back, I can connect events to the depression such as the day Dad came home with a man named Harold. Dad explained he had no home of his own and would live in our basement. Harold helped Dad on jobs and often would peel potatoes for Mom, a job that was now difficult for her. Harold was part of our family for the winter. Without explanation or a good-bye he left in the spring with his clothes in a paper bag.

We were never hungry. Our supper table had potatoes, a can of vegetables and a meat. Preparation for Saturday supper began Friday night when mother put dry navy beans in a pan and covered them with water to be soaked overnight. Saturday morning she'd boil the beans until the skin could be blown off. Then they were drained, put in a pot with mustard, molasses, a chunk of salt pork and enough water to cover the beans. The pot would be placed in the center of the oven for all day cooking. Occasionally, a little more water would be added. The southern belle had learned how to cook Boston baked beans. Saturday was also the night we might have company for supper and company meant hot-dogs to go with the beans and a can of fruit for dessert.

Another Saturday tradition was to help Mom change bed sheets. The top sheet became the bottom sheet and a clean sheet was tucked in on top. Downstairs was also cleaned on Saturday. Scrubbing the kitchen floor meant kneeling on the floor with a bucket of water, a scrub brush and a rag to wipe up soapy water. Once in awhile Dad hid a nickel in a corner. Upstairs was cleaned on Thursday after school so I could help.

Mom became the envy of the neighborhood housewives because she didn't have to empty the pan of water beneath the icebox. Dad fixed the drip with a hose that led the melted ice directly outside.

Dad disciplined me with verbal statements. Mom strapped me once on my bare legs using a leather belt. With each stroke she wept, *"This hurts me more than it hurts you."* Dad who was observing this strapping hung the belt on a nail in the kitchen and said, *"Rosa, it's here in case you need it."*

Obviously, they were a team pitted against a smart-aleck. From that day forth, all Mom had to say was, *"Do I have to get the strap?"*

To earn a living Dad was painting and wallpapering the houses of the rich in Montclair. When he'd arrive home from work I was the one to help unload paint buckets and drop cloths from the truck. It didn't take long for me to learn to have the wind on my backside before shaking the drop cloth.

Often he'd take me on side adventures. One such trip meant parking the truck off the road by the railroad tracks, putting groceries and beer in a box, then, dragging the box down the railroad track. Leaving the tracks we followed a path in the woods that led to a group of shabbily dressed men. One with an amputated arm, one minus several teeth his buddy had pulled with pliers. All came with a hardy welcome for Dad and his kid. The long empty sleeve dangling fascinated me as did the tooth pulling pliers resting on a rock.

I was impressed when the men showed me how to place some grocery items in the nearby brook for refrigeration. I sat on a rock listening in pure joy while Dad and the hobos drank beer and told stories. It was a disappointment when Dad refused their offer of food, by saying, "We have to get home."

Walking back on the railroad tracks he said, *"Poor buggers need the food for themselves. I'm damn lucky to be working."*

I had one pair of shoes that were polished Saturday night for Sunday school. For school I had two identical navy pleated skirts and two identical white blouses Grandma Webb had made. When one considers we had our weekly bath Saturday night and put on a clean skirt and blouse to go with the freshly polished shoes for Sunday...why, that wardrobe was more than ample!

Hannah had identical wardrobes and when she outgrew hers, they became mine. Mother would say, *"I don't understand how Hannah can wear her clothes for two years and you wear them for a couple of months and the seams come apart!"* It was years before I realized her clothes were worn out when I inherited them.

As a child the depression meant nothing to me. I always had a roof over my head, clothes on my body and food to eat. And as Dad would say, *"What the hell more do you want in a day?"*

Chapter 2

ALL IN THE FAMILY

Where we love is home,
Home that our feet may leave, but not our hearts.
Oliver Wendell Holmes, *Homesick in Heaven*

From Texas to California
Keith Severin

My parents had five boys, two weeks less than seven years separating me, Keith, the oldest and Kenton, the youngest. I don't know what Mother had in mind, but we all had names that begin with the letter "K". With the exception of Kenton, we were all born in the Texas Panhandle, in the days of the Depression and Dust Bowl. I was born north of Booker about four miles on the Allie Lehman place. Kenneth, Jim (Jimmy Kay) and Kayler were born east of Booker about four miles on the Teare place. We were all born at home with Dr. Tom Smith delivering us. After we had moved to California in March 1935, Kenton was born in the Los Angeles County Hospital, 14 November 1936. We were living in a little house in an alley in Huntington Park.

My parents, Bernard and Mae (Meyer) Severin 4 July 1927
Clear Creek, Beaver County, Oklahoma

Dad certainly was a reliable and willing worker, all of which meant that while he never had a really good job, he was never without one. In Texas, he farmed – dry land farming, for sure – with horses and milked our several head of cows to have cream to ship. That was our cash money. In California, he picked olives, grapes, and oranges before getting a job at Tingley's second-hand furniture store cleaning used cook stoves. Our rent was then $16 a month. Proving he was a good man, that job led to a good one at Western Pipe and Steel, but that was about thirty miles from where we were living in Pomona. Dad must have rented a room or something in Huntington Park, close to his work, where he walked to work, before we could move there. He moved from El Monte, after Kenneth was killed in a plane crash in July 1947.

Life in the Severin household centered on Mother, who was an excellent manager and ran a tight house, undoubtedly the result of her younger years. Mother's mother died when my Mother was ten or eleven years old, leaving a family of two boys and seven girls. My Mother was the fourth oldest, and when her mother died everyone was still at home except Aunt Grace, the eldest of the crowd. Being the oldest girl at home, everything fell to my Mother to get it done. In effect being the mother for all the younger sisters, housekeeper for her father and older brothers, and helping with the farmwork, my Mother never really had a childhood. And she went to school, got top grades and won penmanship competitions. I believe she even attended some in the first year of college. In a word, Mother had to get things done and she found a way to do it. That, in addition to the genes she inherited from her very strong willed father, made her all the more certain that her way to do things was the only way. As pretty as my Mother was, one would never have guessed she could be or was so tough and determined.

My brothers and I were raised in a way that there was never any question about doing what was expected of us. We rarely had to be told or asked – and then never more than once - we just did it. Mother was the one who used the switch, usually saying, "Go get me a switch"! And it had better have been a good one, because if it wasn't, she would go find two good ones and not stop until they were worn out. If things were really bad, Dad would pull his belt off. That was, I think more of show for Mom. The belt would pop, and we wouldn't get more than a few licks. I remember the last time Dad used his belt on me. Kayler, about five or six years old, had wanted a drink of water from the end of the garden hose and had his mouth over the end of it. I turned the water on full blast giving him a real mouth full. Dad got after me in a hurry.

Needless to say, we didn't have much money. There was no such thing as allowances. Each of us boys found jobs doing what we could to earn something. As a consequence, we are all fair money managers and we know how to work. My first paying job was a magazine route where I delivered magazines to subscribers every week or two, depending on whether they got The Saturday Evening Post, Life, Look, Liberty, The Ladies Home Journal. Once a month I collected from the subscribers. That was when I was in fifth grade. I also mowed Mr. Gaskill's lawn, using a reel push mower. What other kind was there then? I got 25 cents for mowing that lawn. I recall one time I had not done a good enough job and Mr. Gaskill, who lived across the alley from us, came over and told me to come back and do it over. I learned from that.

Because we didn't have much money and had come from a farming environment, we always had a garden, plenty of vegetables and fruit trees, usually some chickens, rabbits, maybe a turkey and sometimes a cow. Mother always canned things out of the garden and made jam from the peaches and apricots, as well as canning them. If we could find a berry patch, that added to the jars on the shelves.

We never wanted for the necessary things of life; they were never scrimped on. On Sundays Dad would take us all for a ride in the car. Often he would drive by the little airport and watch the planes land and takeoff. On the way, Dad would stop and buy a quart of ice cream, a whole quart for the seven of us. Dad would usually go around with his spoon and ask each of us boys what flavor we had.

He was a great man - too good, far too good for his own good!!!

A BOY OF FOUR
Eugene Tucker

My first recollection of my mother placed her in white slacks and a light colored shirt. She had dressed to take baby sister and me to the field down the railroad track, where we had a small truck farm. Mom was a large woman about 140 pounds and stood some five feet eleven inches tall. She was an imposing figure with a strong determined voice which echoed authority. I quickly learned not to question or to challenge her demands. Retribution would be quick and decisive. I was about four years then with no fear or clue about her temperament and resolve. I quickly learned that "stop" meant stop now and not at my convenience. This struggle of wills would continue throughout our lives together. I never learned and she never relented. I was the only son in a family of three girls, one younger and two older. I was the one thorn who dared to stand his ground and question Mom's every move. A few slaps across the face and rear didn't seem to bother me much. I just returned for more as my questioning persisted every day.

Growing up in a house with three sisters and a mother presented many challenges for an only boy child. I was too young to be of any interest to my older sisters and my youngest sister was too little to tussle with. Mom would not permit me to wrestle with her anyway. So, Mom became my immediate target for harassment. After all Dad had to go to work each day and he was too tired to play much when he returned home from his ten hour day at Tie Plant. Tie Plant was a company town about six miles south of Grenada, Mississippi, where many of the men worked treating logs for telephone poles and cross ties for the railroads that were shipped all across the country. This was a plant where physical labor was required to do the heavy lifting of logs to be placed on conveyors for their creosote baths and then to stack the logs when the processing was completed. Dad would return home drenched in creosote. Many would suffer from lung and many other related problems and would linger for years before succumbing to their ills. For this Dad would earn fifty cents to a dollar per week in the early days. Rent on our little two room shanty was fifty cents per month. Mom would take in washing and ironing to supplement Dad's income. Often she would request food in place of money for her work. I don't think we considered ourselves poor, for everyone we knew was at about the same level of existence. I remember our family receiving commodity rations that were handed out from box cars parked on the rails in front of our house. Oranges, eggs and rice were common items distributed here. I heard about WPA projects created by President Roosevelt. I would hear loud air raid siren that would go off daily to alert us of a possible air attack from some enemy. I later learned that the *"Japs were coming"*, so we may have to seek cover, but where? We had no bomb shelter in our neighborhood or even in our town. So, we just looked up into the sky to see if the planes were coming.

Dad would take his usual "bird bath", eat supper, and go to bed to prepare for the next morning sunrise. Mom often complained about having to cook rice for Dad everyday. She called him a "gichy". He would take a full bath in our tin tub on Saturday night. Sometime we would all take a bath in the same water. It was too difficult packing water from the artesian well located in front of the water plant at the end of our dirt road. Water would then be heated in the large black iron pot in our back yard and carried by bucket and emptied into the tin tub.

Our little house was located on Railroad Avenue a few yards from the train tracks. I think there were four sets of tracks that ran from New Orleans north to Rochester, New York. The mile post in front of our house had the number 618. That was the number of miles from that post to Chicago, Illinois. Many would board a train at our tiny station located a short walking distance from our house and head north for a better life. Our family would take this venture some two years later and land in Louisville, Kentucky.

Railroad Avenue was lined with two room shanties sporting tin roofs, a porch, one step and a weathered gray color. A chimney separated the front from the back room and served as a vent for our pot belly stove and our cook stove located in the backroom. The rooms were approximately fourteen by fourteen feet each. There was a front door and a window on the front; a rear door and a small window at the back. A little out house was located at the rear of the compound and served all of the little shanties. Mr. Frank Houston owned this little compound which was separated from the other part of the city by a ten to twelve foot tall wooden fence lined with pine trees that towered above the fence. The paved roads stopped at the edge of the fence with dirt and gravel continuing on through our compound. Railroad Avenue was about a city block long with a row of small shanties on the west side of the tracks; an ice house, a coke cola plant, a juke and Mr. Plummy's house were on the east side of the tracks. Mr. Plummy was a successful bootlegger and lived in a larger and nicer house painted white with green trim. They even had a swing on their front porch. To the north east of Railroad Avenue were the "brick yard" and the cotton gin. Railroad Avenue was my playground for a boy of four. The dirt, gravel, railroad tracks, trains, the tall fence and pines behind our house was the world I knew. We were not poor, because I had some food everyday. I was not even aware of my parents' struggles to survive. After all I was only a carefree little boy with a loving and supportive family.

O'L TOM GOT STUFFED!
Harriet Burgess

He came to live with us one blustery day in March, riding up the dusty lane in the mailman's old Model-A Ford. He shared a big cardboard box with lots of other baby poults—another name for baby turkeys.

You could tell from the beginning he was going to have things his way or else. As he grew bigger he did a lot of strutting around the barnyard and herding the hens about. Grandma always made sure he got the bigger portion of the cracked corn as he was destined to be our Christmas turkey and we needed him to grow big and fat!

As the days crept into fall he strutted and gobbled even more and anyone unfortunate enough to walk past him was promptly chased. He was now weighing about 30 pounds.

Finally on Christmas Eve morning Grandma told Granddaddy to make the trip to the woodpile and chop off Tom's head. Well if you've ever seen a chicken dance around headless you should have seen Tom go into his dance. Blood everywhere!

Later after dipping him in scalding water and plucking out all the feathers, including those pesky little pin feathers, Grandma cleaned and washed him. He finally dressed out to be 25 pounds. By now much of the day had gone by.

After supper the fire was built up in the old wood cook stove and Tom was put in the big roasting pan. Butter was drizzled over his breast and brown paper laid over that to keep from burning. All through the night Grandma basted Tom with the drippings, catching catnaps on the little couch in our country kitchen, which was separated from the house by a breezeway.

Christmas morning was devoted to preparing the rest of the Christmas dinner: homemade rolls, mashed potatoes with giblet gravy, green beans canned from the garden and various pickles and jelly made the previous summer.

With much anticipation the city relatives arrived and gathered around the big dinner table to give thanks for our bountiful harvest.

Tom Turkey certainly did his share!

Chapter 3

DEPRESSION ANYONE

Do what you can with what you have, where you are.
Theodore Roosevelt

THE FLIGHT NORTH
Eugene Tucker

My family was in depression for most of my youth. Life in my little compound in Grenada, Mississippi changed very little since slavery. Dad worked for Tie Plant producing ties for railroads and telephone poles that were distributed throughout the country. Manual labor was the order of the day as Negro men worked in the hot creosote without any health benefit and very little pay. Dad brought home fifty cents a week to feed, clothe, and house his family supplemented by our truck farm and what Mom could contribute through her day work and ironing. We received oranges, margarine with a separate coloring package, and eggs from the government's emergency stockpile. Occasionally, we would receive rice and cheese. These were welcome additions to our food supply. Even though these were surplus commodities from the government, we appreciated the handouts and looked forward to receiving them. Sometimes they would be bartered with other people for a few coins. I believe my Mother had to go downtown to receive food stamps to receive the rations. Most of our neighbors met there at certain times during the month.

I remember the freight trains rolling by in front of our house heading north. Often the freight cars would be parked on the sidings overnight loaded with produce, lumber, cotton, and other cargo waiting to be picked up the next morning or within a few days for the trip north. In the middle of the night some of the men in our compound would raid the trains and make off with sacks of food, oranges, apples, and whatever they could carry. This was a crime that could have resulted in a jail sentence or even death. Hunger overcame fear as the men, women, and children participated in the raid. I don't remember my Dad joining the group and I don't know how some of the spoils got into our house. It was said some of the security people hired by the train participated in the looting. A few hundred yards up the tracks from our house was the cotton gin, where cotton was processed and loaded on the box cars headed north. Negro men from the Brick Yard, a small compound adjacent to the cotton gin and across from the train station, worked here. The cotton gin was operating well into the 1960's. The beautiful white cotton wrapped neatly into bales represented what once was the pride of the south. Even though Negroes now shared in the economy that once made White men wealthy, their wages just managed to sustain them just out of reach of slavery. Sharecroppers faired no better and debt often tied them to their landowners for life. Freedom never reached them.

People in my compound talked about leaving the south to start life over. They heard about hoboes from New Orleans on the trains and landing in Illinois, Ohio, Michigan, and even New York. They heard that Chicago was a boom town with Negroes living in nice houses, wearing fine clothes, and drinking whatever they wanted. Jobs were plentiful and wages good. Members of my family moved to Rochester, New York. My Dad's brother moved to Chicago, married an enterprising woman and established his own tailor shop and cleaners. Men went first to find jobs and settle then sent or come for their families. I remember some of the men returning sporting "sharp clothes, gold teeth, diamond rings, Stetson hats, and black and white wing tip shoes." Boy, they sure looked prosperous! This image gave impetuous to almost everyone in the town. My Dad showed no interest in the euphoria and continued to work at Tie Plant and work our truck farm with our one eyed mule, ADA, until one day Mom and her brother, Uncle Charlie, convinced Dad to try his luck in Louisville, Kentucky.

AMAZING STRUGGLE
Harriet Burgess

I was born in Washington, D.C. and lived there the first four years of my life. My mother and father divorced and I went to live with my maternal grandparents in Fairfax County, Virginia on their dairy farm. At that time my mother had to work and chose a nursing career as there were few choices for women in the workplace at that time. She came to the farm each weekend if her schedule permitted.

Life on the farm during the Depression had its ups and downs. There wasn't much cash but we never went hungry. My grandmother was the dairy farmer—working from sunup to well into the evenings. She could milk the 25 cows as well as any man, which she did twice a day – in spite of a severe arthritic condition. The joints in her hands were badly swollen and stiff and she couldn't bend her fingers—she milked with the cow's udder between her thumb and forefinger, in a stripping motion. As she washed milk cans in the big metal vat in the dairy she often remarked about the relief she got from the hot water on her swollen hands.

Granddaddy was a stone mason and left each day for his various jobs—sometimes 30 to 40 miles away. He didn't drive a car and had to depend on others for transportation. Many times as he would put it, he had to take the "TP&W" (take pains and walk) for the last three miles home from Centreville, his drop-off point. He had a crippled arm which had been injured in a work related accident as a young man—the bone was never reset correctly. This forced him to hold heavy rocks cradled in his left arm while he chipped away with his mallet held in the right hand, as he formed the stones. He was a quiet and gentle man, always nursing an injured duck or chicken back to health there on the farm.

Grandma and Granddad McWorter

My Uncle Sam, Grandma's youngest son, lived with us and was like a big brother to me. Often as a little girl he would let me go with him to the fields when he was plowing or making hay. It was exciting to sit on the big horse and ride back to the house for dinner. On the way we'd stop at the creek for the horse to get a drink. I was always scared of sliding off its back into the water when he bent down. Often I was dogging my uncle's footsteps around the farm. Later when we got a tractor to replace the horses, I would ride along with him, sometimes even falling asleep from the motion of the machine.

Uncle Sam with our bull "Gabriel"

On Sundays in the summertime we often made ice cream for the company coming out from the City. Aunts, uncles and cousins who had jobs in Washington, looked forward to country cooking and family visits.

The ice cream process was hard work and time consuming. We had to travel eight miles to Herndon to bring back big blocks of ice and buy pellet size salt for freezing the mixture. Grandma made the ice cream mixture and placed it in a metal cylinder which had a dasher (agitated the contents) inside that constantly stirred the ice cream and this fit down inside a wooden container. Two inches of space between the metal cylinder and the wooden container were alternately packed in layers of ice and salt, until the top was reached. A crank on the outside of the wooden container fed through it and the metal cylinder and turned the dasher in the ice cream mixture. After cranking for an hour or more and adding salt and ice occasionally, the melted salt water ran out of a small hole in the bottom of the wooden container. Several people took turns 'cranking'. When the crank became hard to turn the ice cream was ready to eat. Our reward came when we tasted the homemade peach or strawberry delight—all the kids would fight over who got to lick the dasher! Peaches that went into the ice cream came from an earlier trip to the peach orchard near Leesburg.

In early spring wild garlic was popping up everywhere in the pasture and the cows were brought in a couple of hours before milking so they could belch off the garlic they had eaten. If the garlic smell got into the milk-- the dairy where we shipped would send it back—there would be no pay for that shipment.

After years of milking cows by hand, we were able to afford a milking machine. It was an apparatus with four rubber lined tubes connected in a cluster which had air running through it and these tubes were held up under the cow's udder, sucking the udder into the tube. The sucking motion of the machine stimulated the cow's bag and she let down the milk which ran along a tube into a large pressurized aluminum bucket. The raw milk (which was unpasteurized at this point) was taken to the dairy nearby and poured into a big overhead vat suspended over a series of refrigerated coils. The milk ran out of the vat and down over the coils which took out the animal heat. How good was the taste of the fresh milk coming off the coils—cool and sweet! The milk was poured into 20-gallon milk cans and placed in a huge metal square ice box filled with water. The box was anchored to the cement dairy floor and held about 20 milk cans. This box had 2-3" insulated walls that contained coils for cooling the water. It was powered by electricity and when the cans were placed in the water it kept the milk cool. We shipped to Chestnut Farms and the dairy company truck came each morning to pick up the night and morning milk supply, carrying it back to the plant for pasteurization and distribution to its customers.

Grandma canned a lot of vegetables from her garden as well as fruit from the various trees and the blackberries that grew in the pasture. Some of the canned food went to pay off the newspaper man who delivered the Washington Times-Herald. Each week our eggs were traded at the general store in Centreville for groceries.

Grandma raised chickens, turkeys, pigs and cows. The crops were put in by my Uncle Sam and an occasional hired hand. Often the city relatives came out on Sundays for a good home cooked dinner. Grandma excelled with her home made rolls, fried chicken prepared in the old iron skillet and vegetables fresh from the garden. We butchered hogs in the fall, smoked hams and made sausage.

Excitement knew no bounds when the big thrashing machine rolled into the yard in late summer. The wheat had reached a golden yellow in the fields and was ready to thrash. The crew set up the machinery near the barn and the wheat, which had been cut and bundled in the field earlier, was fed into the thrasher, traveling along a big wide belt. The wheat was separated from the stalks with the straw going through a chute and piling up on the ground. The grain poured out of another chute into feed bags manned by a worker who tied them off. Grandma once again spent the morning preparing a big dinner to feed the workers.

Later our corn crop was cut and brought in from the field to fill the silo. The tractor powered a huge cutting box with a wide belt running over a fly wheel on the tractor, which formed a loop connecting to the box. The green corn stalks were placed on the belt and fed into the cutting box where they were shredded and blown through a chute into the silo. The shredded corn was converted into silage to feed the cows through the winter. The silo was a circular two-story metal structure for storing the silage. It had three windows at different intervals for ventilation and an outside ladder ran up one side with doors at each level to access the silage when needed. I was forbidden to climb this ladder but every now and then would sneak off and climb it to "look out over the world". A worker stood inside the silo as it was filled and guided the chute around the interior so it would fill evenly. Throughout the winter, periodic checks were made for 'hot spots' in the silage, loosening it up with a pitchfork to prevent fermentation which could cause spontaneous combustion.

Once again Grandma prepared another big harvest dinner. She cooked a big pot of green beans flavored with 'fat back' (a salty fat piece of pork), plenty of fried chicken, biscuits, corn on the cob, tomatoes from the garden, mashed potatoes and gravy, accompanied by pitchers of ice tea. Dinner was served on long tables made of plywood covered in oilcloth, located in the yard under the shade of an old oak tree. The workers ate and rested there for an hour.

My grandmother was a woman of many talents, sewing various items from the flowered feed bags that chicken and cow feed came in. She made aprons, dresses, pillow slips and even bed sheets—though a bit on the rough side—they were quite pretty.

My grade school years were spent on the farm where I attended a country grade school at Floris Elementary, about eight miles away from home. There were no black children attending—they had their own school near Pender—further down the road. Riding a school bus for miles along rough country roads, (many of them dirt), until you got home, made a long day for a small child.   A bright spot to the end of the long day

Grandmother in one of her 'feed bag' aprons with a pet calf

was listening to favorite radio programs (i.e. Jack Armstrong-the All American Boy, Stella Dallas and Orphan Annie) while the family was out in the barn doing the evening milking. After supper, Grandma would pour over homework with me while I shed many tears over arithmetic—which I hated. Even though she always had the right answers, her method of arriving at the answer was different from our teacher's, and I would get in trouble at school later!

In the winter we heated with a pot-belly wood stove in the living room—undressing downstairs at night and running madly upstairs to jump into bed—reversing the next morning to dress warmly by the stove again. All the cooking was done on the big old Home Comfort wood stove range in the kitchen which was separated from the main house by a breezeway porch—the old wooden kitchen had burned down many years ago. We practically lived in this room with its big round oak table and settee in the corner.

For Thanksgiving and Christmas, Grandma put a 25-30 pound turkey (which she had raised) in the wood stove and spent the night basting the bird, between taking naps on the small settee. All the family would come home for the holidays to enjoy the good food (especially the fruit cake which had been aging for weeks) and to celebrate the season.

On freezing winter mornings the water pipes outside the kitchen would freeze and Granddaddy had to light a kerosene soaked rag wrapped around a stick and hold it under the pipes until they thawed. These pipes supplied water for the kitchen.

Life on the farm was hard but rich in love. The memories are precious.

I WAS AS RED AS THE COAT
Thelma Webb Wright

During the depression Dad often said, *"We're lucky. We have plenty to eat and a roof over our heads. What the hell more do we need?"* Clothes were not a priority. In late fall he must have realized winter was on the way and my older sister, Hannah (12) and I (10) needed a coat. Dad came into the living room holding two winter coats that Mom had worn for several years. He handed Hannah the beautiful, bright-red coat that had a white, fake-fur collar and specks of black and white in the red fabric. With joy, Hannah tried in on, and it fit her. She was now the proud owner of the coat I had always loved.

Dad then reached for the ugly, gray coat with narrow stripes of brown woven in the fabric. It had wide cuffs that ended with big, pointed wings sticking out. There were two patch pockets on each side, one opening above the other, and a big, wide belt with a huge buckle. Even folded over, the collar sat high on the shoulder. I hated that coat whenever my mother wore it.

Dad held it, *"Thelma, try this on."*

It was a baggy fit until Dad wrapped and buckled the wide belt around my waist. I glanced at Hannah smiling in the beautiful, red coat that fit her perfectly.

I stood in the baggy coat and proceeded to have a temper tantrum. *"I don't like it. I hate it. I won't wear it. Why can't I have the red one?"*

When I exhausted my tantrum, Dad calmly said, *"The red one fits Hannah, and this one fits you. If you don't like it, you don't have to wear it."*

That last sentence made me feel better until he added, *"A coat is only good for one thing and that's to keep you warm."*

Dad hung the coat in the front hall closet, and the subject was never mentioned again. He had given me the choice to wear or not wear it. In silent anger I thought, *"I am not going to wear it."*

However, when the snow came, and icicles hung from the gutters, I changed my mind and wore the coat...without the belt.

Dad's work of painting and paperhanging was always slow during December. The day school closed for the Christmas holidays was the day we would depart for our annual visit to Grandma and Grandpa Webb's in Lake Worth, Florida. Preparations for the journey, as in previous years, began the day after Thanksgiving when Mom started packing. What few clothes we had disappeared piece-by-piece in cardboard boxes. By departure day, the only clothing we had left was covering our bodies.

The packed boxes were stacked on the back seat by the right window. Hannah sat in her red coat by the left window, and I squeezed between her and the boxes wearing a sweater, not the ugly coat. My unspoken choice was not mentioned by anyone. There was no heater in the car. Mom and Hannah wore coats. Dad and I wore sweaters. Dad had no coat.

Another subject not mentioned was my tendency to be car sick.   Really car sick! When we reached U.S.1, Mom made her annual statement, *"Now we stay on this road all the way to Lake Worth. It starts in Maine and ends in Miami."*

We didn't get out of southern New Jersey before my car sickness was ready to be realized. I leaned toward the front seat grunting with a mouth full trying to attract Dad's and Mom's attention.

Hannah ordered, *"Sit back and stop moving around."*

I turned toward Hannah-my mouth opened and showered the beautiful red coat...fake-fur and all. Hannah screamed, *"Thelma threw up on me!"*

Dad pulled to the side of the road and Hannah, still yelling, got out dripping with vomit. Dad stepped toward me and gently wiped my mouth with his handkerchief. Then, turning to Hannah he attempted to clean her coat saying, *"She didn't do it on purpose. Stop your fussing."*

Hannah, Dad, and I returned to our seats. Dad started the motor and Mom, who stayed in the car uninvolved, said, *"I'll open the window a crack."*

When I think back, throwing up on Hannah and the beautiful, red coat is one of my happiest childhood memories.

(Because Mother had Parkinson's Dad often played the role of a mother.)

Chapter 4

AT WORK AND PLAY

The highest reward for a man's toil is not what he gets for it, but what he becomes by it.
Author unknown

The Way Things Were
Eugene Tucker

In the early 1930's many of the men in my family and among our neighbors had left the farms and were working in mostly unskilled jobs throughout our town. Dad worked for Tie Plant, an employer of many Negroes in Mississippi. Tie Plant provided cross ties for the railroads and poles for electric companies. One day one of the foremen brought and exhibited the leg of a Negro man who had been lynched the night before. The leg was later thrown into the fire that heated creosote for processing the cross ties. Dad's first name was changed because one of the White men had the same name. Dad became known as "Gene," a label he would carry the remainder of his life.

Men found work at the box factory a few miles north of Tie Plant. My oldest sister's, Eunice, husband worked there producing a variety of boxes from plywood and were loaded onto box cars that were parked on railroad tracks for shipping north. There was an ice house on the east side of Railroad Avenue where we lived. Several young men worked there, including Mr. Plummy Watts' son, who died in an accident. Mr. Plummy was a successful bootlegger. A large block of ice fell on his son and was not discovered until it was too late to save him. Ice produced here was delivered to houses and businesses throughout the town. Our ice box could hold a twenty five pound block of ice for several days before it all melted. We didn't need much during the winter. Uncle Windom worked at the saw mill located a few miles northwest of Tie Plant. He would later work and live out his life in the company town of Tie Plant, Mississippi. Uncle John, Mom's oldest brother, left the farm where he had been a sharecropper for most of his life, and joined the road beautification crew planting trees along Highway 51. After Uncle John's wife died and the children left home, he had to leave the place where he frequently referred to as slavery. He was never able to break even at the end of the year. He would say *"They worked us to death and we got nothing!"* Highway 51 connected Memphis, Tennessee to Grenada, Mississippi and south to the Gulf passing through Jackson, Mississippi. This would be the highway where James Meredith, would travel escorted by US marshals in his effort to integrate the University of Mississippi in 1962 as the country watched and survived a bullet wound en route.

Working in hot creosote, logging, railroads, highways, saw mills and the fields were employment opportunities of Negroes here in Mississippi. Strength and endurance were important attributes. They were in no position to bargain for wages and benefits. Business owners could get the work done for only a few dollars per week. Jobs requiring the intellect were not available to Negroes in this town. This was our town.

Women worked for White families caring for their children, cleaning house, and cooking. When my mother returned to Mississippi from Little Rock, Arkansas, where Grandma had relocated the family a few years after Grandpa left, she would be hired out to a White family until she ran away to live with Grandpa. Grandma had sold the farm, rented two box cars, packed her belongings including two Model T Fords and moved to start a new life in Arkansas. Mom was fourteen years old when she went to live with Grandpa following her brief stay in Arkansas. Mom went to work for John Borden, the owner of the Borden Company, a New York Stock Exchange company. Mom recalled that Mr. Borden was a short man who sported riding habits, an equestrian hat, and carried a whip. Mr. Borden had come to Mississippi to *"buy out the south"*. He established a dairy farm on a place called Glen Y, where Mom worked taking care of the Borden children and learning to cook the northern style. There were many people hired to tend the grounds, manage the Holstein cows, groom the horses and ponies, and help his wife around their estate. She said he was a kind man and handed out tips generously, so people were always eager to be near him and respond to his wishes. The man who would meet Mom and become my Dad worked here tending to the polo ponies and prepare for the frequent games that were held here. Mom remembered receiving many hand me downs from Mrs. Borden.

Before Grandma moved to Little Rock, she would *"rent out"* her girls to White families for a fee. The girls were outfitted with a change of clothes and a pair of shoes and delivered by wagon to *"your White folks"*. Grandma collected the fees. Mom recalled having to ask for permission from her employer to go home for a short visit. She had to walk for miles with no shoes because the ones she had were too small and worn. Upon arrival home Mom asked for a pair of new shoes where upon Grandma admonished her for leaving her *"White folks"*. Mom had to borrow her brother's shoes because Grandma refused to buy her new ones. Grandma returned Mom to her place of work and returned to take her home when it was harvest time. This would be repeated until each child became bold enough to escape. Grandma would eventually return to Mississippi without fanfare and without much of her fortune. According to Grandma's sons she would entertain her friend, Tobe Williams, lavishly with fried chicken, greens, sweet potatoes, freshly baked hot rolls, cakes and pies, and best homemade wine. She served them the left over chicken heads and feet. They would sneak around behind her back and steal fried chicken from the molasses bucket that hung from the rafters and one day they got intoxicated from the homemade muscatel wine. For this they were severely scolded and threatened. This did not stop them. They were infuriated with the situation and as they aged sought refuge with Grandpa. Grandpa had left the old farm citing *"A good walk is better than a bad stand."*

A 1960'S WORKING WOMAN
Harriet Burgess

In 1947 I entered the Federal Government service with the Department of the Interior in Washington, D.C., working first in the Office of the Secretary and later the Bureau of Reclamation and finally the Bureau of Indian Affairs. A government job was a secure place for a woman at that time. Under the civil service we earned sick and annual leave, health insurance and a retirement plan. The working conditions were excellent and Interior covered many interesting programs throughout our country, (i.e. Bureau of Mines, Geological Survey, Bureau of Reclamation, Fish & Wildlife Service, National Park Service, Bureau of Land Management, and the Bureau of Indian Affairs.)

Author working at Bureau of Indian Affairs, 1970s

In 1948 I married my husband, Jim, and we started married life in a one-bedroom apartment in Southeast Washington, D.C. Our first son Jimmy was born in 1952 and I continued working. My husband worked for the Post Office Department in the Air Mail Facility at National Airport and we commuted to work together. Our second son Johnny was born in 1954 and we moved up the street to a two-bedroom apartment. We had a good baby sitter nearby for the children and we dropped them off on our way to work each day and picked them up on the way home at night. Later when my husband was assigned to the night shift it fell to me to drop off and pick up the little ones.

After eight years of city dwelling a longing for the country life surfaced and a loving grandmother gave us five acres next to her farm. We moved out to Chantilly in Fairfax County, Virginia where we built a new home. (In the 50s you could put up a three bedroom rambler for $15,000 if you put in the well and foundation yourself, which we did.)

Our $15,000 home in the winter of 1958

In January 1958 our daughter Margaret Ann was born in one of the heaviest snow storms to hit that area in a long time. We had to keep her in a baby carriage near the fireplace for warmth since the new storm windows hadn't been installed yet; we had only just moved in the new house after living at my grandmother's farm for a year. Now our clutch was up to three. My husband had transferred his job to the Air Mail Facility at Dulles Airport, which had just been completed, and I still commuted to D.C.—a 20-mile trip one way. The commute from Chantilly to D.C. in the 60's was a breeze compared to the nightmare it has now become. We were able again to secure a wonderful baby sitter for our children and as they got older she put them on the school bus each morning and met them in the afternoon after school, keeping them until we returned from work.

We had a huge garden, about ½ acre, and supplied the neighbors and friends at work with our produce. We even canned tomatoes and froze corn and string beans. Lots of weekends we had cookouts in the backyard with friends and family.

Our kids attended the local schools and as they grew older they had part-time jobs while still in school. Jimmy worked at the local golf club picking up golf balls and also acquired a never ending passion for golf to this day. Johnny worked at a Corgi dog kennel and got to attend an international dog show for Corgis in New York State where he worked with the dogs. Margaret Ann worked in a dress shop and later worked for an auto parts store. They all married later and we now have eight wonderful grandchildren.

The Department of the Interior, where I worked, offered many outside activities through the Recreation Association, which also gave discounts at local stores. We had a credit union which offered a good interest rate on savings accounts and reasonable terms for financing a car. The credit union was there for the employees and did a lot of business. We had a woman's softball team, of which I was a member, a men's softball team, golf teams and a bowling league. A dance was held once a month in our cafeteria, complete with orchestra and a revolving glitter ball. Every summer the Recreation Association sponsored a field day at Ft. Hunt, Virginia for the employees and their families. There were races for adults and children, contests, (i.e. tug-o-war, golf driving, horseshoes, and lots of picnicking.) The mounted Park Police gave demonstrations jumping their horses through hoops of fire, which thrilled the kids. The highlight of the day was the Miss Interior beauty contest where the contestants appeared in bathing suits and were chosen from girls employed at Interior.

There was not always smooth sailing at the Interior Department. When I changed my job to the Bureau of Indian Affairs, we moved into a building across the street, located on Constitution Avenue. In the 1970s a militant group of Indians, (American Indian Movement, known as AIM), decided to take over our building, protesting various injustices they thought had been done to the Indian people by the Bureau of Indian Affairs. They did not speak officially for the Indian people but were doing their thing—and boy did they do their thing! The work force was evacuated from the building one afternoon and the AIM group moved in, destroying everything they could lay their hands on, (i.e. typewriters thrown down stairwells, curtains pulled down, furniture broken, papers and files littered all the offices and halls; generally overall destruction throughout the building.) A huge wigwam was erected on the front lawn of our building and became quite a sightseeing attraction. No one wanted any violence against these people so the situation remained for well over a week while negotiations went on and finally some of the demands were met. We moved back in and the cleanup process began. It took weeks to get things back in order and the expense to the government for this takeover was immense.

Many happy vacations were spent with our family 'heading west' to visit the national parks, Indian reservations and many other points of interest that took our fancy. We camped most of the way starting out in a 1950s 8-passenger Plymouth station wagon; the boys slept in a tent at night and mom and dad and little Margaret Ann slept in the wagon with folded down seats. Later we worked our way up to a Ford Falcon pulling a second-hand wooden camper. We planned these vacations for months ahead and the kids still talk about those trips and our adventures.

In 1976 the Concord began flying over our house once a day on its approach to Dulles Airport—it was a grand sight to see. We would all run out in the yard to watch it approach. The FAA had installed a bronze plate in our front yard to mark the highest elevation in the airport area. At night some of the planes approaching Dulles Airport on the north-south runway had their approach lights shining in our bedroom window.

In the 80's Chantilly had gone from a small crossroads to a well known location on the map. After living in our home there for 32 years, our world caved in when the county rezoned us from residential to industrial and quadrupled our taxes. Farms had all been sold and developers moved in with office complexes. Our ideal world came to an end and we had to sell the last remaining acres of a family grant that dated back to the 1700's and prepare to seek new ground.

We moved to Fauquier County where life seemed to be saner and the countryside looked like Chantilly in the old days. My husband and I both retired from the government with 32 years of service apiece and we built a new home in the foothills of the Blue Ridge. Life was great once more and we enjoyed the leisure life and the grandchildren nearby.

My husband died in 1996 but I live on at home and share a lot of my life with the grandkids and their activities and do a bit of traveling. Life is still good.

The Blizzard of 1996
Helen P. Hannett

Our home in Foxland Village, just outside the Town of Warrenton, is a winter house. It sits up top of a sloping hill which makes for wonderful sledding when it snows. There are high winds there too that make for large drifts, perfect to make snow houses and snow tunnels with. There are even clear views of the storm fronts moving in that we can see from our window. This house comes to life when it snows.

So we were ready for the big storm, even festive about it. We had, so we thought, amply stocked with food—including milk and bread, logs for the fireplace, and choice new library books and magazines before the blizzard of 1996 hit Saturday evening. One of our children accompanying me to the supermarket joked that it looked like people were getting ready for a war.

By late evening there was a blanket of snow covering the frozen branches of the trees and the ground. By morning we were snowed in.

All snowed in

Our seven kids are always happy about snow days, thrilling to the thought of transforming our steep but sloping one-acre front lawn into another Snowshoe Mountain. Two nights of nonstop snowing with this blizzard, kept them (ages 8 to 23 years) in a flurry of activity building their sled run. A lot of time and tremendous boyish energy (five boys to be exact) was spent packing it with jumps. Then they iced it up with water and let it sit for several hours. This first one they called Viper Run.

We have your basic flat sled—seven of them. One was neon pink, the others were neon blue. They are rectangles of bendable plastic with oval holes at one end for handling that store easily together flat. I providentially bought them all last year and put them away. These sleds make my kids very happy. I caught the second youngest sledding upside down head first down Viper Run on one of them. My oldest son sat down on one of those sleds and went down Viper Run for a midnight sled ride with his dog Bubba. Bubba came back in afterwards covered with snowflakes up to his ears.

As the snow kept falling, our kids tooled a second run. It started about 40 feet from the other one on the same upper level but near a far end of our house. This new one was built to curve around, aerodynamically using the rises and falls of our lawn. It swerved around and joined Viper Run midway. For hours at night, the 16-year-old was dousing it with buckets of water to slick it up. This second addition was named Cobra Run because the two runs form the shape of a raised cobra's head to the rest of the run—the long snaking body.

The beauty of this I was told by my smiling eleven-year-old is just missing collision with the other sledder who is coming down simultaneously.

Jumping on a sled and sailing down our packed and iced steps and flying across the sled path, engineered for increasing speed, was one of the highlights of the winter of 1996 for us.

I have to tell you that six of our kids took two breaks (time outs) while building the Viper Cobra Suicide Run. They had to take turns shoveling 4½- to 6 ½-foot tall snowdrifts from our 200-foot-long gravel driveway, and they had to shovel wide enough to accommodate our full-size cars. On his own and without suggestion our 19-year-old also shoveled our back sidewalk. My husband went out with the kids after lunch and they shoveled until 7 p.m. It was a beautiful job done 99 percent by the kids.

On Tuesday our neighbors needed help shoveling out, so two of our boys, the 19-year-old and the 16-year-old, helped shovel their deeper and steeper, winding driveway. It took them three and one-half hours to do it. Afterwards they again worked on their sled run, still exhilarated and tireless.

A stack of Scientific American magazines totally captured the attention of the older boys for some time. The youngest two children and I enjoyed reading many library books together.

By Tuesday night we were out of the hundreds of dollars of stocked food. We had to scrounge through every neighboring supermarket for what we considered essentials. Unsuccessful and still in a gala mood, for the next two days we treated ourselves to soda pop and cookies as substitutes for milk and bread!

I had come back from the store unsuccessful in a further search for bread and milk when my husband told me more snow was expected for the next two days. Since our kids would probably be out of school all next week, too, he arranged to purchase HBO and CINEMAX channels to keep the kids happy at home.

The next day I suggested to my kids that they build a snow tunnel, ice house or maze over the bottom end of the sled run to make it more fun. They told me, "Do you know how much work that takes?" They watched the new movie channel all day. They told me they were too tired. And that's when I curled up with a new novel and relaxed.

Chapter 5

COMING OF AGE

Childhood, whose very happiness is love.
Letitia Elizabeth Landon, *Erinna*

LIFE WASN'T ALWAYS A 'BED OF ROSES'!
Harriet Burgess

My life underwent quite a change as I entered the teen years. My mother had remarried and I had a new stepfather. I had left the farm of my grandparents where I had lived throughout my grade school years. I was living in an apartment in Arlington County, Virginia. I went from a country school atmosphere where I had known my classmates since first grade to a huge metropolitan school with strangers all around me. Being on the shy side I didn't make friends readily.

My stepfather was a cold, aloof man and had been an only child. Though he tried to do the right thing, he didn't come across as a substitute father. He was a scholarly type –his mother had been a school teacher in Colorado. He was always giving me IQ tests to see if I was on a level with Arlington schools. Needless to say we never did really bond. He died about four years later.

After completing junior high school at Thomas Jefferson I moved on to high school at Washington-Lee. By then I had formed several close friendships in the neighborhood and life was looking bright.

My mother worked for the government and we still were on a very limited budget. In fact she rented out one of the bedrooms of our two-bedroom apartment. It was wartime and rooms were at a premium with a lot of 'out of town' people flocking into the area in defense jobs.

I can remember at 16 I got my first pair of silk stockings and also had my first machine permanent. I went from long pigtails to short and curly. The perm was an experience in itself. Your hair was divided into little sections and a hooded machine was rolled over to the chair and individual clamps were pulled down from inside the hood and fastened to each clump of hair. These clamps had wires leading back up into the interior of the hood and when the motor was turned on it sent heat to the hair. You had to have the timing down pretty good or you would end up with frizzy hair—which I had several times.

My spending money was earned babysitting for 15 cents an hour and that would get me to the Buckingham movie house once a week where the admission was l5 cents also. Another pleasure during those teen years would be a trip into D.C. on a Saturday afternoon for a show at the Capital Theatre on F Street, complete with stage show, newsreel, cartoon, short subjects and main feature. You could spend the whole afternoon there in that beautiful theatre which looked like a palace. Washington, DC had several lovely theatres in that general area which were elaborate—the Palace, the Columbia, the Earle, and Keiths. I would hit them all in time, depending on what was showing.

In my junior year in high school I got a summer job in the personnel office at Ft. Meyer, a military base in Arlington. This was my first introduction to the work world. I had to walk past the jail each morning on the way to my office and the inmates would all whistle. I really dreaded that walk! The next year my summer job was in Washington, DC at the Dept. of Commerce.

In 1945 I graduated from high school and enrolled in George Washington University in D.C. After two years I decided it was not for me-- I wanted to earn my own living. I got a job with UNNRA (United Relief & Rehabilitation) located up near Dupont Circle. The job was great and I had a certain amount of freedom even though I still lived with my mother in Arlington and paid her a sum each week to help with expenses. It was fun to stroll down Connecticut Ave. at lunch time and having my own money I could buy some of the beautiful clothes in the shop windows.

At UNRRA we had invitations to many embassy functions which were quite elaborate. I remember one reception at the Iranian embassy in particular where quite a few of my co-workers attended. We had a lady supervisor named Sylvia, who was a real dragon and cracked the whip over us there at UNNRA all the time. Everyone on this particular evening had on their best 'bib and tucker' and upon entering the foyer there was a beautiful marble staircase which led up to a second floor area where there was a wet bar and a buffet dinner set up along a side wall.. As the evening wore on the crowd became more animated as will happen with an unlimited wet bar. Toward the end of the evening when we were down in the foyer getting our wraps, Phil, our supervisor's husband, tumbled down those marble steps, dead drunk. Things were rather subdued in the office next day with supervisor Sylvia.

I worked there at UNNRA until it was disbanded and then entered the federal government at the Department of the Interior. I never forgot my country roots and most weekends I went back to the farm to visit the grandparents.

NOW WHAT?
Eugene Tucker

It was June 1953 when I walked down Chestnut Street towards the church where the Baccalaureate services were being held for my high school graduating class. What a day this was! The sun was very high in the cloudless sky. Trees and flowers were exhibiting their finest styles and colors as butterflies and bees searched for nectar. I do not remember why I was walking alone. Usually I walked with Leona, my baby sister, who was graduating too. Perhaps, she was meeting some of her friends. Today, I had no books under my arms. I was dressed up in my slacks, carefully starched shirt, necktie and jacket. I did not wear suits often because I could not find one with a 38 inch jacket with extra long sleeves, and pants with a 28 inch waist. I could find slacks in the boys department, but without a matching jacket. This dilemma would haunt me for many years to come. So, I wore my outfit proudly as I walked and reflected as I often did when I was alone, sometimes having an open conversation with myself. The conversations often became quite loud when I thought no one was around to hear me.

This was the first graduating class from the new Central High School. What an exciting moment for our city and the children from around the region. Our class had moved into this beautiful building during our senior year. We had spent the previous three years in the old Central High, an old converted hospital with iron see through stair wells, dark gray corridors and overcrowded classrooms, which had once served as hospital rooms and nurses stations. The new Central was a modern structure with large classrooms, a beautiful auditorium, an intercom system, wide hallways, and wonderful lighting throughout the building. We even had a large gymnasium, a football field, a track, and space for an Olympic size swimming pool. Athletics was a big deal at our school. The swimming pool was not installed. School administrators would not permit it to be built because none of the white schools in the city had a swimming pool and it was thought not appropriate for an all Negro school to be so equipped. The pool has never been built. Central High was the only public high school in the city of Louisville, Kentucky for Negroes and it served the city and all of the near by counties. Bussing was the only way Negro children from the county could attend high school. There was one Catholic High School for Negro children whose parents could afford to send them there. However, many changes were beginning to take place in our town. One could feel the uneasiness and undercurrents of discontent among people in my community. There was talk about integration, equal treatment under the law, and upgrading of neighborhoods. As I walked along Chestnut Street I began to reflect and relive some of the moments that had affected my life up to this important day.

This was the year when St. Xavier High School, a white Catholic High School in the city, decided to play our school in football, basketball, and track. St. X, as it was called, was one of the best schools in the region both academically and in sports. They had won many state championships and had a proud tradition. The city was on edge when the first football game between the schools was scheduled. We were coached on how to behave and reminded about the importance of this game to the future of race relations in our community. I think every student in the school and many who had long since graduated attended this "game of the century". We proudly displayed our gold and black school colors and cheered with every play. We lost a close hard fought game, but demonstrated that we belonged on the same athletic field with the state champs, even though we just recently had a practice field with decent facilities. However, when St. X, the reigning state champs in basketball, scheduled a game against us, they would soon learn that they were no match for the Central High basketball team. Everyone in the city looked forward to this game. Many thought that the Negro kids were too undisciplined to compete against the state champs. Our coach was the brother of the coach at Tennessee State College, the dominant basketball power among black colleges and universities for many years. Their styles of coaching were quite similar--a dominant center position, good ball handlers, and an outside shooter, with emphasis on execution. This would be a game to be remembered! We were the champs among Negro high schools throughout the state. And now we were to face the "real champs of Kentucky high school basketball.

I sat in the stands as president of Central High's Student Council wearing a letter on my gold colored sweater that I had won for my exploits on the track team. I had won this letter in competitions in Indiana and I had lost a duel with a St. Xavier miler. I was reserved as usual, but churning inside for the big game to begin. There was Sammy Moore at center standing about six foot six inches tall and known for his left handed hook shot. Sammy would go on to star at Tennessee State University, perennial champs among Negro colleges, and then to star with the world famous Harlem Globetrotters. Then there was John "Pie" Livous, a lanky six foot four inches playing guard. These two players remain in my mind although each member of the squad was a star this night. The game began with high expectations from both teams. We gained the opening tip and immediately scored on an uncontested lay up. The crowd went wild! The struggle for acceptance for the Negro in this state of Kentucky was on. St. X was no pushover, for they had sent many players in all sports to major colleges throughout the country, so they settled down to the task at hand. However, St. X had not played against players with the gift of quickness, athleticism, skill, and a desire to be respected as those from Central High School. "Pie" Livous would take a step across the center court line and sink his shot. St. X thought it was a fluke and left him alone until they realized he could hit his shot with ease and consistency. So, they sent two players out to guard him. Central responded by sending the ball inside to Sammy Moore, whose hook shots were a thing of beauty, as he glided across the foul lane, issued a head fake and sank the shot. St. X had no answers. They soon realized they were not going to defeat this team of Negro players. As I sat there in the stands full of pride and wonderment, I had no idea I was witnessing history in the making. This game would change athletics in the state of Kentucky forever.

For years there existed a rivalry in basketball between Kentucky and Indiana. No Kentucky all star team had beaten an Indiana all star team. Every year Indiana had a majority of Negro players on its squad and handily defeated the Kentucky all stars. The pride of the state of Kentucky was on the line and when the scouts and coaches witnessed what had happened in this game, they decided it was time to add a Negro player to the all star squad from Kentucky. Their decision was rewarded with their first victory ever over Indiana and the Negro player from Central High School was named the star of stars for the game. This was the first time they had seen a player tip in a missed shot from the free throw line. Central High would later be permitted to participate in all state athletic competitions following the 1954 Supreme Court decision on integration. Central would dominate the game of basketball in the state for years to come until bussing of white students to achieve integration of schools was ordered. Children from our old neighborhood were bussed to the county and white children from the county were bussed into Central High. It was not long after this that our best athletics were scattered throughout the city and county. Winning state championships would become a rare event and in the year 2003 Central High is on the extinction list. It now serves no purpose for city administrators and the land it occupies is prime development property. So, a school with a long history and tradition for the city's Negro citizens and one that had become predominantly White in the late twentieth century must now lose its link to the past.

As I continued walking and talking to myself, I remembered the first party I attended. I must have been about sixteen years old and one of the girls that I had a crush on had a birthday party. No one knew that I was even interested in any girl especially her. Most of the invited guests were older than I and had more experience at such things. The young men gathered outside trying to garner enough courage to go inside and confront the girls. Someone had gotten a bottle of whiskey and was passing the bottle around for each of us to take a drink. I knew this was not for me. My life would be in jeopardy if I went home with the odor of liquor on my breath. So, when it was my turn to drink, I stuck my tongue into the bottle and turned it up as if to take a big drink and quickly handed the bottle off to the next person. Everyone thought I had taken a drink and applauded with approval. Imbued with our new found courage we went inside. The song of the evening was "The Tennessee Waltz". What a beautiful song. I took my place in the nearby corner and watched others dance and took my sheepish glances at the evening's celebrants. As the years passed I learned this beautiful young lady for whom I had a crush had married one of her suitors at her birthday party that night and had mothered several children. Boy, am I glad the lyrics had sent me a message on that evening---"Since I lost my baby..."

As I continued my journey towards the church everything around me was beautiful but I did not notice much. All of a sudden I felt a warm sensation on top of my head that caught my attention. A bird flying overhead had dropped me a message as if to say "wake up and smell the roses". What was happening here, I wondered? Is this some omen? Had I forgotten to be humble and thankful for all the good things that had happened to me? I had no time to contemplate the answer. I quickly took out my neatly starched handkerchief and wiped away the dropping from my head and continued my journey. No bird poop would hinder the excitement of this day.

Now I was wondering about my senior prom. So much talk and planning was taking place around me. I had no special girl friend, and I was not interested in Clenteria who was always in my house trying to get me interested in her. She was trying to get my mother on her side, but Mom was not interested in mating me with anyone, even though she was friendly with the girl and knew her family. After all we had grown up together. I finally got the courage to ask a girl who said yes. Just before the prom she decided she would rather be with her boyfriend who had gone to Vietnam. My prom night was spent listening to my date moan for her boyfriend. Clenteria, my sister and her date, who was a member of my singing group, spent the evening together. After an hour of listening to my date, I decided to take her home and return to the prom.

It was fashionable to spend the night out, have breakfast at some all night place before returning home. We found a diner on Walnut Street, now known as Mohammad Ali Boulevard, named after the world famous boxer and a graduate of Central High, and had breakfast. My parents did not seem to worry about our being out all night. They had trusted us all these years and now it was time to let go. After all Baby Brother and Baby Sister were out together and for the final time as high school children. I heard Mom ask

"I wonder what does the future hold for my two young children?"

This question would be answered in time.

The Holy Father Is Passing By
Helen P. Hannett

On August 30, 1953, my future husband had just turned seven, when he saw Pope Pius XII outside Rome in Castle Gandolfo. His father, a U.S. Army officer, was stationed in occupied Heidelberg, Germany with his family. My husband's father, mother, and their three children took a train from Germany to Rome. They left Germany in the dark hours of the early morning. My husband remembers going through a long dark tunnel in Switzerland and also seeing a man on a bike racing with the train down a hill then easing up after reaching the foot of the hill. When the train stopped in a town in northern Italy, his father got off temporarily to pick up lunch for his family. He was so delayed obtaining it, that he almost missed the train as it continued on. Once they arrived in Rome, they took a bus to Castle Gandalfo, the Pope's summer residence out in the hills where it was cooler. As Pope Pius XII was blessing the crowd from his balcony, a photographer snapped a picture of that moment with my husband as a little boy in the square below sitting up high in the crowd on his father's shoulders. What an exciting experience for him!

On October 16, 1978, shortly after white smoke arose from the Sistine Chapel smokestack to inform the world that a new pope had been selected, a member of the College of Cardinals came out on the balcony and announced in Latin the election of Karol Wojtyla. In St. Peter's Square below and worldwide there was an initial moment of uncomprehending hushed silence as we heard his difficult Polish name being pronounced for the first time. It took time to translate the full name of "Karol Wojtyla" from Latin to the vernacular.

Karol Jozef Wojtyla had taken the name Pope John Paul II, in memory of his immediate predecessor, Pope John Paul I who had died after only 34 days as head of the Catholic Church. John Paul II presented himself for the first time to the faithful below in St. Peter's Square. He was the first non-Italian pope elected in 455 years and the first Polish pope, and it was love at first sight.

The morning of October 7, 1979, about a year after his election, Karol Wojtyla, our new Holy Father John Paul II, was in Washington, D.C. After first stopping at the Shrine of the Immaculate Conception at Catholic University, he would visit Trinity College down the street on Michigan Avenue. At Trinity College, founded in 1887 as the first Catholic women's college in the United States and run by the Sisters of Notre Dame de Namur, Pope John Paul II would first preside at an Ecumenical Prayer Service at our Notre Dame Chapel, which had won the Gold Medal for ecclesiastical architecture in 1925. After finishing the prayer service and departing Trinity's Notre

Dame Chapel, he would then drive further into the campus to Kerby Hall for the Blessing of the Sick.

Trinity College had sent out invitations to all its graduates in the Washington, D.C. metropolitan area of which I was one, inviting alumnae and their families to the enclosed campus outdoor standing areas for the visit of his holiness John Paul II. Enthusiastically, we gratefully accepted my school's once in a lifetime offer.

My husband, the human alarm clock, who regularly rises with military precision, woke us around 5:00 A.M. that morning in order to secure the best place at Trinity from which to see the pope. We had four children then and were expecting another. We decided to take along only our oldest son, who was about to turn seven and was in second grade preparing for First Holy Communion.

After our dark haired high school babysitter arrived, we drove from our northern Virginia home to park our car at the Pentagon just across the river from Washington, DC. We took the metro from there to Brookland, which is a community near Catholic University. We walked from the metro stop to Catholic University, and for a minute considered walking up the stairs of the Shrine, but the Holy Father was there already talking to a vast number of people. As we walked on, I twisted my ankle on the sidewalk. I would pay the price later for not putting ice on it. Then we turned into the enclave of Trinity College.

For three hours we stood in the grassy circle edging the circular driveway opposite Trinity's Notre Dame Chapel. We wanted to be close enough to get a good look at Pope John Paul II. To hope for anything more than that would be improbable because of the thousands of people on the streets and the numbers of people who now stood with and behind us.

My look alike high school and college classmate, Paula, joined us. We had both called each other earlier. Paula and I were both part Polish. She was also part German. With a flower in her hair, castanets click-clacking, and gypsy skirts flying, she had toured Europe as a flamenco dancer after our graduation from college. We met coincidently for lunch one day on her return, and she sat us down breathtakingly in the middle of a table of young handsome businessmen. Ever since she had taken a summer acting program during high school from Father Hartke, who had taught Helen Hayes, at Catholic University, I thought she had started pushing the envelope on the possible. We were both married now and were mothers of children of similar ages.

When Paula said, "We have to move closer," I followed her, leaving my husband with our son high on his shoulder on one side, and crossed the driveway to the other side. Now we were in the first line of people whose feet, including ours, touched the sidewalk from which the Pope would exit the chapel. We stood together on the sidewalk opposite the members of the Board of Trustees. The Holy Father in his white papal robe left our Notre Dame Chapel, walking under the triangular pediment of the sculptured relief of the Madonna and Child. He stopped in front of Paula, who spoke a few words in Polish to him; then she took his picture. When he turned to me, I preferred to touch him—shaking his hand warmly. He looked into my eyes with so much love and kindness that I can never forget.

When we received the next issue of the *Trinity College Alumnae Journal* in the mail, inside, several photographs illustrated the Papal Visit. There was one particular picture that was amazingly similar to my husband's childhood photo but bigger and closer up. It was of my oldest son sitting up high on my husband's tall shoulders. They were standing with many people around them in about the third row away from Pope John Paul II, who was in the foreground. It is much like a similar one, much like that one my husband cherishes of himself with his father and Pope Pius XII in 1953.

As for me, I chose not to take a picture with a camera but used my eyes and heart instead. That way, I would not miss any of that grace and light of the heart, mind, and soul that photos often hide. And now the hand that shook the hand of our most beloved Holy Father John Paul II is sending this story to you!

Chapter 6

EDUCATION

The more you think you know, the more you realize how little you know.
            Eugene Tucker

A SIMPLER TIME AND A SIMPLER PLACE
Harriet Burgess

An education was considered an important goal throughout our family over the generations but often there was not the money to pursue the higher levels.

My maternal grandmother, born 1882 in rural Fairfax County, Virginia was taught by a governess at the old home place called Leeton. As she got a little older she was sent down the road to Cabells Mill, three miles away, to be schooled with several neighborhood children. Here she was introduced to Latin, French and the classics. The rest of her unmarried life was spent at the home place learning young lady skills, cooking, needlework and some work in figures, since her father was a lawyer and a gentleman farmer.

When my mother came along she attended a little one-room schoolhouse three miles from her home for her grade school years. She, along with two brothers, had to walk the three miles in all kinds of weather, carrying a brown bag lunch. When she got to high school age she was sent off to Hampton-Sydney College in the Shenandoah Valley, (around 1914), to live with an uncle who was president of the college there.

He tutored her in Latin and other subjects for a while to prepare her for admittance to Mary Baldwin Seminary for Women in Staunton, Virginia. Religion and Latin were emphasized strongly here. After graduation she went into training to become a nurse at Emergency Hospital in Washington, D.C.

My school years consisted of a country grade school through the sixth grade at Floris Elementary, (Fairfax Co. didn't have a seventh grade in the 30's). I still remember most of those teachers. Miss Katie, my first grade teacher, was a heavy-set motherly type. I can

My mother Margaret in nurses training at Old Emergency Hospital, Washington, DC, 1920s

remember a yellow and black polka dotted dress she often wore. She would hug all the kids and make over them. The third grade teacher, Miss Lucas, was sharp-nosed, stern and waved her ruler at us all the time over the arithmetic problems, which I hated and did poorly in. Miss Tavener in the fourth grade was kindly, and fun to be with. (She later taught my children in grade school and lived to be in her eighties.) My all time favorite was Miss Stauffer in the sixth grade. She was pretty, single, easy-going, and taught the glee club, of which I was a member. Grade school days have many fond memories.

Author in first grade at Floris Elementary School, Fairfax County, Virginia

On the first day of May each year a Maypole was erected in the school yard. The little girls in the first and second grades had costumes made at home out of crepe paper sewn on over a petty coat to resemble daffodil petals. In the afternoon all children and their parents would assemble in the school yard for a program and the little girls would dance around the Maypole holding onto ribbon streamers attached to the pole, interweaving among each other as they circled.

Once a year we had a school play and the parents came to view it. My big moment came once when we enacted the death of Julius Caesar. I was given the part of an old witch and my grandmother had made my costume out of a burlap bag. I approached Caesar and uttered the words "Beware the Ides of March, beware!" I was so proud of that part—it was my brief experience on the stage. Grade school days have many fond memories for me.

In 1938 I entered Junior high school in Arlington, Virginia, where I picked up the seventh grade through the ninth at Thomas Jefferson Junior High School. These were unhappy years, adjusting to city life, a new school, new friends, and a new stepfather.

In 1941 I started a whole new life at Washington-Lee High School, also in Arlington, where I rode the commercial bus line from my Buckingham apartment. For the most part the teachers were great: Ma Mallot in English, loved to talk about 'Cleo and Anthony' which spiced up the subject. There was one 'dragon lady' teacher who taught typing. She had very black hair pulled back smooth and tight and never cracked a smile. She flunked me in that class so I made it up in summer school, little realizing that the rest of my working career would involve typing. I became quite proficient in it. High school was enjoyable, even though the country was deep into World War II.

High school graduation, Arlington, Virginia

After graduation, I entered George Washington University to study journalism. I really never got too enthused over my studies there and yearned to get out into the business world and make my own living. After two years I dropped out, and attended Strayer Business College for some brush up courses. I then entered the Federal government and began my long career.

I have no regrets regarding my education, but I sure hope the grandchildren go on to higher learning. Out of the eight, three have graduated from George Mason, the University of Virginia, and Virginia Tech. The rest are hopefully going to continue on when they get to that age.

EDUCATION, A PRIORITY?
Thelma Webb Wright

In my family education was not a priority, nor did it seem to be a priority among the kids in my 8th grade class. In fact, 8th grade was decision time for one's future, so much so that we had a formal graduation ceremony. The girls wore long dresses they made in their home economic class...all the same style from the same bolt of fabric. Sameness didn't bother us. We were excited to have a new dress and our first long dress! Boys wore the best of whatever their family could assemble which resulted in lots of fashion variety. We were a bunch of kids from families struggling to survive the depression.

Our graduation even had speakers who lectured about our future, which had to be decided by graduation day. Boys could go to a boys' vocational school to learn a trade and the girls could learn domestic work at a girls' vocational school. The other choice was to go to high school and ride the bus twenty miles one way. High school offered two programs, college prep or general courses.

I thought I was too dumb to even think about college...that was for the rich kids. My father had a 5th grade education then and became an apprentice to a well known artist. Mother had some grammar school. They did not encourage education one way or the other. I was on my own. I hated school, saw no need for an education and barely passed.

On my sixteenth birthday I quit school. The law allowed me to and so did my parents. Dad said, *"Get a job!"*

With ten cents I boarded a bus to the large town of Montclair. I had no master plan in mind. I walked down a street and passed a hat store that displayed a help wanted sign in the window. In the thirties women wore hats and a new Easter bonnet was a necessity, if you could afford one. This was April and Easter was only two weeks away and the hat store needed help to sew labels in their creations. I could thread a needle and clip thread with small scissors so the job was mine!

On the Saturday before Easter Sunday I was no longer needed and was released from my first job. I was so insecure I never asked for my pay. Obviously, I was not prepared for the work world!

My next job was being a mother's helper. That paid five dollars a week for a full eight hour a day of changing diapers, heating baby bottles and preparing dinner for the couple. The only thing I knew how to prepare was a baked potato, then, heat a can of peas or string beans. Dessert was a can of room temperature fruit. By the time they tired of a baked potato, can vegetables and a can of warm fruit I was fed up with their ugly, screaming, wet bottom baby. They found a replacement and I walked happily away with my last earned five dollars.

My brain must have been coming out of the moth ball closet because I was thinking this was not the way to, as Dad had said, "Get a job". Fortunately, Dad had been hired by the Colonial Williamsburg, Virginia organization, to be in charge of their paint department. On my seventeenth birthday we were unpacking our belongings in a Williamsburg bungalow.

I had lost interest in the work world and decided to check the local high school. Talk about a gift from Heaven! Williamsburg kids graduated from high school in the eleventh grade. Why, I could do that last year and be graduating the same year as though I had not quit school in New Jersey were twelve years were required. So in 1942 I sat on stage with cap and gown and received a high school diploma! The only thing I can remember about my senior year at Matthew Whaley was we had the day off for Robert E. Lee's birthday. I didn't know who he was or why we celebrated his birthday. I didn't care...it was a day off!

We were newly involved in World War 11 and Williamsburg had become a sea of service people from the Navy, Army, Marines and C.B.'s. I applied for a job at the small telephone company and because I had a high school diploma I was hired and trained as an operator for $12.50 a week. I loved the job and was good enough to be advanced to supervisor at $19.00 a week. Education was paying off!!

I became aware of the advantages of an education and proceeded to take courses in community colleges, then regular college...any course...art appreciation, ceramics, English, writing. I was like a sponge wanting to absorb every drop of education I could find. I even attended college while my kids were growing up.

There were problems concerning my going to school as the children were growing up. John was not encouraging me in anyway; in fact, he felt I was neglecting my family duties. I didn't accept this as neglecting my family as the courses were in the evenings. The children were not latch key kids. My favorite course was Interior Design. I was determined to pass the mid-term exam and I studied hours. I even taped information so I could listen as I peeled potatoes. I was nervous when the test was given. A week later the results were handed to us. My grade was a shocking A+. I was so excited I couldn't wait to reach home to tell John. I phoned him from the school, his words are etched in my memory, *"The teacher gave you that grade to make you feel good because you are the oldest in the class."*

I wept all the way home. There was no further mention of my A+.

I completed all the night classes that would lead me to a degree and it was time to attend day classes. I signed for the classes, attended a few and then gave in to John's argument that I was now neglecting the home and family. There would have been a few latch key days for the children. I accepted the guilt trip and stayed home.

However, I brain washed my kids as to how they were going to go to college, no questions asked.

My school teaching daughter tells me, she knew it would be grammar school, high school and college, period. I smile when she says that.

My youngest son rebelled about not needing or wanting an education beyond high school. I drilled into him he could do anything he wanted in life...after he received his college education. After his graduation he phoned me from a fishing village in North Carolina, *"Mom, I just want you to know I am earning my living on a shrimp boat shrimping and I am the most educated shrimper on the boat."*

Well, the "shrimper" returned to college and became a wonderful licensed architect.

My oldest son, who would sneak a flashlight to bed and read, read, read, graduated from the University of Virginia and has created a happy life breeding dogs.

Not long ago, my daughter, now in her fifties, asked me why I had insisted she was going to college. I answered, *"You came home from your first day of kindergarten and said, 'When I grow-up I want to be a teacher.'"*

The larger truth is, I did not want my kids to know the disadvantages life would give them without an education. I did not want my daughter to ever hear her husband say, *"I am the one that has an education, you don't have one."* That remark would conclude any opposing conversation. That's a hurt I did not want her to carry.

As for me at age 81...I keep on learning... the sponge has dry areas that need to be moistened with new knowledge.

And what I have done with some of my do-it-yourself education?

I taught ceramics to the delinquent girls in the Bon Air School. They were girls in trouble and needed encouragement to make better choices in their life.

I developed a program for the city of Richmond, Virginia, to place foreign visitors into local homes so they could learn about the United States and we could learn about their countries. This was during the period the south was going through desegregation. This program received world-wide recognition.

One of my college courses led me into a position of interior decorating for an expensive furniture company.

I helped to establish a travel agency in Richmond.

I opened my own quality craft shop in Lancaster, Pennsylvania. I should have concentrated on more bookkeeping courses in school, because the shop failed financially. In self defense, it was 1976, when the Legionnaires' disease attacked Philadelphia and killed tourism which many of us in Lancaster were depending on.

The most fun education gave me was the opportunity to teach Seniors how to write their memories...oh, I have also had two books published. "Grandma You're Lopsided" and "Tramp Artist."

EDUCATION AND FREEDOM
Eugene Tucker

When I was a young boy everyone told me how important it was to learn to read, write, and compute. My elders often said,

"I didn't get much book learning, so I don't know much". "I wished I had more learning!" "Boy, you better stay in school!"

The only learning they got was from reading the bible and discussing it among each other. My grandfather learned to read and write his name this way. Usually one person, who became a minister and learn to read and write, would attempt to teach others. A Minister could generate a following in this manner. The bible became their text book. It seemed that learning to compute and reason came natural for most of them. My mother recalled the one room shanty where they went to school for part of the year until it was time to harvest the crops. All of the children who were large enough to work would have to help in the fields. She recalled children from one family would come to school with baked rats packed in their buckets for lunch. They were often teased by the other children. Tattered clothes, bare feet and pigtails were fashion trademarks. Mom had to wear a pair of her brothers' shoes on more than one occasion. The teachers could barely read themselves, so what you learned was minimal. However, they were able to plant the seeds for the pursuit of knowledge for many of the children. Some of the children paid little attention and came only because their parents forced them. They did not see from the conditions around them the connection between spending time in school and the chance of a better life. The ones who came were grouped by age and the teacher would try to give some attention to each group during the day. My Uncle Charlie often said most never got out of " Ned in the first Reader." Mom learned to read and write here. She advanced to the eighth grade. However, her desire for learning was insatiable. This would be her pursuit throughout her life as she continued to read, question, listen, challenge and expand. Dad taught himself to read, write, and compute. His knowledge of geometry still amazes me today, since he had very little formal schooling. His brother, who remained with his family in Big Black, Mississippi, graduated from high school and became a tailor and dress maker owning his own business in Chicago. This was quite a feat for someone from this place. Grandma was a skilled thinker and learned from the school of hard knocks. She could not be cheated in any transaction or confused by rhetoric. I observed my uncles, aunts, cousins teaching and instructing each other. None of them were satisfied living in the darkness of ignorance. These were the 1920's and 30's and schooling of Negro children was not important to southern Whites, while the US Congress continued to grapple with the issue that began before reconstruction.

Here we are in the twenty first century and the slogan is "leave no child behind." Now this includes all minority groups, including Black Americans. Black people watched and participated in the Industrial Revolution producing enormous numbers of inventions and innovations to the workplace and expanding the knowledge of the universe, making advancements in science, medicine and technology. They overcame poorly equipped classrooms, inadequate facilities, and often poorly prepared teachers. Their thirst for knowledge could not be suppressed by would be oppressors. To many knowledge was freedom even though they may have to sit at the back of the bus or be turned away from signs which read "Negroes need not apply". I witnessed many of the older children in my neighborhood who went off to Kentucky State College, Tennessee State, and other Negro institutions throughout the country, earned degrees and returned home to jobs in the post office or to hotels and restaurants. Education did not seem to matter, but the challenge to pursue knowledge was a constant cry heard throughout our neighborhoods. For me, the act of learning put me in touch with the universe and all the wonderful things I saw in nature. The beauty of shapes, forms, structures, and textures all helped me to create my own reality. I cherished this in literature, art, arithmetic, and mathematics. They were all linked in a sophisticated harmony and the excitement was to dissect it and reveal the beauty contained therein. Books would facilitate my exploration and help to satisfy my quest for knowledge and understanding. School would be the place where I would learn the process of reasoning to be followed by an understanding of what it means to be free.

Chapter 7

The 1950's and 60's

"For the times are a-changin"
Bob Dylan

The Struggle
Eugene Tucker

Changes in my life came often and quickly during the decades of the 1950's and 60's. I began to understand and accept manhood even though I continued to be known as baby brother. Baby Sister, my best friend and confidant, would get married leaving me to fend for myself. This would be a dramatic moment for me as my senses and observations would turn to the world around me. My sister was not there to help me sort it all out. There were daily grumbling about racial inequalities, freedom, voting rights, integration of the schools and housing. Negroes wanted to sit at the counters at Walgreen Drug Stores, try on clothes at Stewarts Dry Good Store, and ride on city buses in non restricted seating. I could feel the tension, but I did not internalize its meaning. I had heard these discussions all my life and nothing had changed. What are these people making all the fuss about, I would ask myself? I did not realize that I was in denial about my status as a Black American. I had forgotten about being ignored while trying to submit an application in the Snelling and Snelling employment agency. They informed me that they could not accept an application from me because their clients had no interest in my kind. I had forgotten about being denied a seat in a Chinese restaurant in Suitland, Maryland, or the many times I was denied housing in Virginia and Washington, DC. I had seen children dragging their mattresses into and out of their shabby row houses when I walked past these houses on my way to the Library of Congress on Capitol Hill. I was employed and sought by employers needing my exceptional talent. I had forgotten that I was born in, perhaps, the most dangerous place in the United States for Black people. I had convinced myself that knowledge would be recognized above a person's color. This assumption would be tested over the next decade and for decades to come.

One day in early 1960, I turned on my small television set and before my eyes were the images of Black men, young and old, women, children, and the infirmed being confronted by angry mobs of policemen armed with hoses, billy clubs, and vicious dogs and mocked by raging White citizens determined to maintain the status quo. The screams of these little children and old Black women touched my very being. They were there asking for recognition of their humanity and for the rights they had earned through the blood and sweat of their African ancestors who had been held in slavery. I quickly realized that these brave people were also there representing me. I was well aware of the efforts of Dr. Martin Luther King, Jr. and his followers. My temperament could not accept his strategy of non violence, I thought. At the same time I realized that the alternative would be a disaster. I continued to live on the margin of freedom.

The images of violence kept coming each day with greater intensity. Sit-ins were met with arrests; marchers were met with violence; white sympathizers were met with murder. White vigilantes roam the roads at night to render their brand of justice for those seeking justice in this land of laws. I continued to see the justice system fail the victims and let the perpetrators go free. *"These were only law breakers receiving their just due, so why punish us patriots who were preserving our heritage"*, echoed the voices of many White sympathizers. The stories I heard as a child sitting at the feet of my elders began to take on renewed meaning. I found the courage to join the March on Washington and stood by the calm waters near the Lincoln Memorial and listened to Dr. King give his famous speech. What an orator and what a message to a nation in racial turmoil! This would be the only march I would join. I could not support sending women and children to face the imminent dangers of the law and the angry mobs.

Then, there was the assassination of President Kennedy in Texas, followed by the assassination of Medgar Evers in Mississippi and strings of heinous killings throughout the south. Dr. Martin Luther King, Jr. would be the next target in Memphis, Tennessee. One evening while I sat in my efficiency apartment on third and F Street in Washington, DC, my favorite news program was interrupted for the network to present a special bulletin.

"We interrupt this program to report that the noted Civil Rights leader, Dr. Martin Luther King, Jr., has been shot in Memphis, Tennessee as he stood on the balcony of the Lorain Hotel."

For the next few hours I sat in the darkness of my room waiting for the fateful news I know would come. During those intervening hours many of the experiences of my life flashed in my mind. The world stood still. Civilization had been dealt a death blow! My champion for freedom had been felled by a coward, a hired executioner, a symbol of repression and white supremacy. The symbol of freedom for Black people would be no more and the cause for which he worked so diligently would surely be silenced for all time. There was no other man in the world capable of carrying on in his tradition. So now the Black race would be without a spokesman. We were thrown back into slavery. Oh, God! Where do we go from here? I mused. Perhaps, the races would polarize or the Black race would at last unite against segregation. The still of night, and the turmoil that erupted soon after the news of his death provided few answers. The rudder was gone. The ship was capsized. The stride towards freedom had run aground and the beacon light at the harbor would not lead the Black freedom ship safely home.

In my gloom filled room I recalled many of the conversations I had with my parents and elders. The days of my youth were filled with stories from yesteryear which contained the aura of a Shakespearian tragedy, or the tales of Mark Twain. Whether the story was light and humorous or whether it depressed the spirit the message was usually the same--God help us. While I sat there many questions evoked my imagination. Can the Negro really leave this matter in the hands of God? After all God was given to us by those who used His precepts to justify our servitude. Is this not a contradiction in purpose? But God is love. Had we done something to displease Him for all time? When are we to be free from this curse?

My parents have not been fortunate to know freedom and present generations are faced with a dim prospect. Yet, we must proceed, for destiny calls and our hearts are desirous of freedom. A transformation in the history of race relations took place in Memphis on that evening in April. Many Black people who had lived aloof in their guarded security found themselves at odds with their consciences over the plight of their Black brothers. White America was aroused too if only for a brief moment before returning to their pre-reconstruction philosophy. But, the doors to state houses, the White House, and the congress were now ajar. Freedom must come to the Black constituents or America will be set asunder. A new Black man had emerged as if from a long stupor. The submissiveness of Booker T. Washington was over. The divisiveness that plagued Marcus Garvey was nearing its end. And now the appeal to the moral conscious of White America lay dead in Memphis. Like a mighty catalyst the abominable news ignited the desire for freedom in every Black man who walked the streets during those days that followed. The reign of violence would continue. Presidential candidate and brother of a slain President would lose his life in California to an assassin.

A SLEEPER
Keith Severin

The decades of the 50's and the 60's are indeed memorable ones. I was 20 years old when they began and 40 when they ended. Lots of things happened in the world that affected me, and I will say that I took advantage of the many opportunities they offered.

The Korean War started June 26, 1950. I was twenty years old, Barbara and I had been married 9 days, and I was going to summer school to finish my Bachelor's degree at the University of California at Davis. Barbara was entering her senior year. Having finished my degree in General Agriculture, I did practice teaching of Vocational Agriculture at Dixon High School the semester after we were married. I have a vivid memory of teaching "vo-ag" youngsters how to castrate pigs. We worked a litter of pigs that belonged to my master teacher's son.

I had been a "sleeper" (volunteer) at Davis City Fire Department the year before, going to school for $30 a month and saved $400, doing yard work, so Barbara and I could buy our own house when we got married. It was a 16 foot house trailer, parked in Slater's Court, and I was the gas man for the trailer park, so we got our bottled gas for nothing. Besides working and saving money for our house, I had carried 18 units the first semester and 20 the next. I got one C and the rest A's and B's. I was so organized and had to be. And that year before we got married Barbara lived with the Dean of the College and his wife, doing the cooking for them. Admiral Chester Nimitiz was one of Dean Ryerson's wartime buddies and used to visit the Ryerson's. Sometimes the admiral would ask if Barbara would make cornbread for dinner. The year before that Barbara lived in South Hall, the women's dorm on campus, and I lived on the Pierce farm west of town. I did farm work there for my room. At that time there were 1,100 students at Davis—1,000 men and 100 women.

Having flown from Alameda Naval Air Station to Pearl Harbor in a Catalina flyingboat, we were in Hawaii on our first wedding anniversary, on our way to American Samoa. We were there from June 1951 until June 1953. Eisenhower and Nixon were president and vice president of the United States while we were there. I helped provide agricultural training to US Samoans Marine Corps veterans who were on the GI Bill, but most of my time was managing the experimental farm and dairy. At first, we lived in "the station", the Naval Station in Pago Pago, and then moved to Fale Suka (The Sugar House) which was on the west of Pago Pago. It was hard and interesting work, but a pretty idyllic life for a young married couple. *"Faifai lemu, fa'a Samoa"* (Take it easy in the Samoan way.)

Back to the States, the Korean War was still going on in mid 1953. I had the opportunity to buy into a dairy in Lake County, California. So, I bought 35 heads of cows and got the place rent free by repairing and cleaning it up.

About the time of my 24th birthday, late November 1953, I got the letter from Uncle Sam. At that time you could be drafted until you reached the age 25. In January 1954, I went into the Army and was stationed at Fort Ord, California. After Sixteen weeks of basic training I went to Fort Holabird, Dundalk, Maryland for Counter Intelligence Corps (CIC) school. I could have stayed on at Fort Ord and worked on the golf course that had been built for the commanding general, "Bourbon" Bob McClure, since I had helped prepare and seed the greens and was seen to know something about lawn care. Since the war in Korea was still going strong, everyone took care not to get crossway with the cadre.

After CIC school, I was offered the opportunity "to go back home", to the field office in Los Angeles, where Barbara's parents lived and where I maintained my legal address. Not at all interested in that, I asked what other alternatives might be. An opening in the Army Language School (ALS) at the Presidio in Monterey in French, "but you may have to go overseas afterwards", so, off to Monterey and ALS. About 7 months of fulltime French, never had tougher schooling, harder work, more expected of me in my life. Very satisfying, though, and I still get along pretty well today *en francais*. My son Kenneth was born while we were at Monterey. He was born at Fort Ord on March 7, 1955. A $7 baby, Barbara going into the hospital Monday morning and I bringing her and Kenneth home Friday afternoon. I was permitted to miss Friday afternoon parade inspection for that, permitted by my lieutenant only because the infant was a son. *"If it was a girl, she could wait until after inspection."* He told me when I asked permission to go get Kenneth and his mother.

June 1955 saw me in Germany, in Offenbach, outside Frankfurt. Barbara and Kenneth joined me in July. Gratefully, I was able to convince the brass that I would be more help if I could learn the German language, so in September I went to Oberammergau to study German and attendant subjects. We lived the first house down the hill from the kasern where the school was located, rented a room there from Frau Beinhoetzl and shared the kitchen with her and her daughter. Barbara would wash Kenneth's diapers and hang them on the line outside where they would freeze. I did well in the German class, studied very hard and had to live *auf deutsch*. I started not knowing any and ended up top of the class of 24 students. Herr Rudnitski was a good teacher.

December 1955 back in the Frankfurt area, but only shortly, since I was assigned to the CIC field office in Bremerhaven. Again, we lived with a German family, the Pusts, rented one big room from them and again shared the kitchen and bath. Barbara, Kenneth and I were getting more and more everyday German all the time— Kenneth especially since he was a blond headed boy with blue eyes.

My work in Bremerhaven was very interesting and grueling too. At the time, many refugees from Germany and Eastern Europe were applying for emigration to the United States. Their applications and background statements had to be verified, and that's what I did. Most of the cases took to the British Zone, to that part of Germany just west of the border of the East German border—the Soviet Zone. On occasion, I would spend 3-4 weeks in the BZ working cases that could be heart rending, and rarely meeting anyone who spoke any English. Some of the questions were tough, very personal. And then having to take fingerprints too was strange. "Only criminals have their fingerprints taken." Lots more was learned about the Germans and about life outside of places touched by the United States. But, everyone wanted to go there.

In late 1956 we were beginning to think about the end of my being in the Army, going home to the US. But, with all the things going on in Hungary, would I be discharged, would we be able to get home? We sailed from Bremerhaven in mid-December, spent Christmas on board ship, Kenneth just a little fellow kept in a harness and on a leash on the rolling deck of the ship on the North Atlantic in late December.

December 31, 1956, New Year's Eve, I got my discharge from active service. It was signed by a Major whose last name was "Liberty"!

Then it was off to Stanford University to do graduate work for a Master's degree at the Food Research Institute. All went well there, in very large part thanks to the GI Bill. The MA degree came in June 1958 and we left for Washington, DC. While we were at Stanford, in October 1957, the Soviets put Sputnik in space, and that was to influence my life and activities for a long time.

I Never Got My Muscles Back
Helen P. Hannett

One lazy hot day in 1950 my little brother Michael, my mother, Dad (a military physician) and I were having a picnic at Salada Creek near Fort Sam Houston in San Antonio, Texas. My little brother and I were sitting on the red wool plaid blanket with fringe that we always used for picnics. I thought the wool blanket itched too much in the heat.

Salada Creek was our favorite place to go for picnics. I remember some medium size trees sparsely arranged and scraggly green grass. The creek was shaped like a parallelogram and appeared like a finger of a small river with lots of water.

There were other military families there that day. Frequently, our neighbors the Summers from Wheaton Road at Fort Sam, would join us there with their household of children. Their children were about ten years older than we were. They would play with us, and that would be enough to hold our attention. But I can't remember them being there that day.

We had finished eating, and I found myself sitting on that itchy red blanket with my brother beside me who was playing with a toy car to the left of me and oblivious to anything else but the car. We were sitting in the clearing about thirty feet from the water with trees in the distant left. The light of late afternoon was coming from the right and behind me at a 45 degree angle. It was getting a little cooler, and so, I was feeling better.

My attention was providentially drawn out to the water, and something kept my eyes riveted there. A little girl had gone out into the creek, but there was a sudden drop off of the shore, and she was drowning. Her father, a big muscular man jumped in to save her, but now he was drowning, too. He couldn't swim.

There were about thirty people there that day. Most of the women were dressed in light cotton sleeveless dresses or pedal pushers. The men wore shorts. Mom was talking with some ladies about twenty feet to the left of Mike and me. Dad, shirtless in the heat, had been cleaning the barbecue grill that he had used and was close to the water. When he saw what was happening, he knew he had to act quickly or he would lose them both. He waded and then dove into the creek.

I didn't think Dad with his scarred up back was fit or that he had any muscles. He once had muscles. He ran on the track team in high school and at Tufts University he was a Golden Glove Boxing Champion. He had a lot of muscle in Fort Ontario in New York, where he trained for was in thirty-five inch deep snow. *"But after the POW camps"*, Dad said, *"I never got my muscles back"*.

I didn't realize till after I had taken a senior life saving class when I was twenty, how dangerous it was to try to save two drowning people at once. In life saving class we learned to only jump in as a last resort, after looking for something like a pole to use for them to grip. Even one person latching onto their rescuer could pull him down, causing a multiple drowning. Dad was a good swimmer, and kept his head above water while he swam freestyle. He kept it above water so as not to lose sight of the people in trouble. First, he swam over to the young girl and got her safely to the shore. Then, he went in after the father and brought him to shore. It happened so quickly that most people didn't seem to notice what happened, or else the picnickers were just frozen with fear.

Dad in his military uniform

Afterwards, Mom came over in her blue sundress with her dark hair up off of her face to check on us. I went over to her, needing to verify from another witness what I had seen and asked her, *"Did Dad save those people?" Yes"*, she responded looking in my eyes, *"Dad was able to make the rescues"*. So that confirmed in my mind that I hadn't day dreamed it. And, it felt good to have shared the incredible experience with her.

Later in the evening after the last rays of sunlight had left the sky and dark descended, Mike and I lay back on our blanket to look at the sky. I hadn't ever seen a sky like this before or ever since. It looked like the whole Milky Way had exploded with stars in front of my eyes. It was like billions and billions of stars—a cosmic event. It was like someone poured thousands of jars of glitter and silver stars as far as the eye could see.

I wonder now if we were gathered there to see some astronomical happening, and if that was the reason for our picnic that late Sunday afternoon and evening. I am sure Daddy had planned for us all to be there to see a forecasted heavenly occurrence or just to see the celestial bodies. Texas skies usually were clear of clouds and thereby perfect for star gazing.

The rescue picture in my mind I would think about nearly every day of my life. It was the only picture I had personally of him saving a life. It meant jumping in with your whole self, getting your arms and legs and brain into the thick of the action, and by the power of your spirit getting them to safety.

The picture of the Milky Way has been whirling around in my head almost as astonishingly as that mental picture of Dad in 1950. It was like God's grand finale after Daddy's successful rescues and I was such an eager appreciative audience. My brother, who had been playing with toys next to me, doesn't remember anything about the day, as he was only about 21 months. I felt like I had been given a great gift that I witnessed, looking both away from me and then upwards to see each event.

SURVIVING
Thelma Webb Wright

Flags, white flags by the dozen flapping in the breeze on the clothes line every day for eight years. Sometimes the breeze would freeze them stiff, sometimes there would be rain water dripping from the bottom edge. Stiff or dripping, they were doomed to hang until the hot sun dried them.

These were my pregnant years which produced four babies, the oldest being of kindergarten age and can you believe, I felt guilty not paying the teacher for baby sitting!

The war for the United States was over. My war for personal surviving was beginning, in a small, very small two bedroom bungalow, bought with the G.I. Loan. The Government Loan meant no down payment required for a veteran. The fifty dollars a month for the mortgage payment was a struggle. How many sleepless nights did I have wondering how we could ever pay off an eight thousand dollar mortgage!

Life in our first home, in Richmond, Virginia, was the introduction to the reality of what everyday marriage was. The neighborhood of young vet families was producing what came to be known as Baby Boomers.

I contributed three boys to add to the one daughter born during the war. My first step into reality was diapers...diapers...and no washing machine and no Laundromats. Yes, there was a diaper service who would deliver to the door a clean supply once a week in exchange for a bag of soiled ones. Nobody in our neighborhood could afford such a luxury. The home remedy was the bathtub and a clothesline in the back yard. The yucky ones were swished in the toilet before they were dropped in the bathtub. However, if they were really, really yucky, they would accidentally be flushed into the city sewer line. When the flags were dry they would be folded to proper size in the peace of the evening after supper when all the babies, had been fed, diapered and asleep for the night. At least, I hoped it would be for the night, but it never was. One and sometimes two would want special attention.

I lived for Friday and Saturday nights when my husband would do the night shift and I could have undisturbed sleep. Aw, sweet sleep until Sunday evening when I'd return to night duty.

Another reality of raising the baby boomers was feeding them. Glass bottles had to be sterilized; then, formula was mixed and funneled into the bottles. Gerber's baby food had to be heated and spooned into open bird like mouths.

The family groceries were purchased in a large grocery store, meat was cut to order, there were push carts to hold the groceries, but no seat to accommodate kids. Shopping was a social event as the store was mostly adults. Friendships developed because many of us were on the same routine...meaning getting on the street car for ten cents, riding several miles to the grocery store, gathering our weeks supply, then with a dime, phone for a taxi at the public phone located in the store. The taxi charge was fifty cents to return me home to a waiting family. Daddy was the designated Saturday baby-sitter.

There were no cars parked in our neighborhood. We all knew how to drive and had a legal license; we just lacked the funds to purchase a vehicle. We waited seven years to save the down payment of five-hundred dollars to buy a second hand jeep station wagon, which the kids named, Bucky. It was a suitable name, Bucky, bucked.

Most wives of the 50's and 60's stayed at home and managed on a weekly allowance which covered groceries, the milk bill and miscellaneous. Mine was seven dollars and whatever I could save was all mine to do with as I pleased, this was known as pin-money. Another way to add to the pin- money was to save empty soda bottles, haul them to the store and receive a couple of pennies for each bottle returned. On a seven dollar a week allowance, I didn't have many soda bottles to return. My pin-money account might have grown to a few penny Tootsie rolls for the kids.

During the war factories were working 100 per cent for producing war needs, thus household appliances as well as automobiles were not manufactured. After the war production began on automobiles and home products, but there was a long waiting period for items. I was on a waiting list for a washing machine. When the arrival of the automatic front load Westinghouse washing machine arrived at my front door I felt I had found the pot-of-gold at the end of the rainbow! My Westinghouse was the second washer delivered in the city of Richmond!

About the time my pot-of-gold was delivered and in use twice a day, the next door neighbor received a small black and white T.V., which offered three channels from morning until late evening, then, it went blank. Most programs were live. The fun was to be watching when a performer would make an obvious mistake. Our neighborhood now had two exciting events for entertainment- My Westinghouse and the next door T.V.

They would take turns to sit in my tiny dining area, look into the kitchen and view the washing machine in action. "Look, the clothes are going around. Look, the water is draining out, now it's spinning the water out of the clothes and look, clean water is going in and now it's spinning the water out. Can you believe it?"

My Westinghouse had competition with the neighbors' T.V., especially on fight night when the neighborhood males were shoulder to shoulder in their living room. As these items became available, the neighbors purchased their own washing machine and T.V. We all started to live in a new life style.

Before ending this vignette of life in the 50's   I feel I owe a dedication to the automatic Westinghouse washing machine. A number of years later when we were living in New Jersey, we had to buy a new washing machine. I watched when it was delivered and being installed and started to cry.

The installer said, "I've never seen a woman so pleased to have a new washing machine she cried."

Through tears I wept, "I don't care about the new machine. The one you are taking away raised my kids, washed all their diapers, has taken care of the family for years, and it was the second machine delivered in Richmond after the war. And it can't be repaired anymore."

Thus, my connection to the white flag period of my life ended.

THE END OF CAMELOT
Harriet Burgess

I remember November 22, 1963 as if it were yesterday. I was working at the Department of the Interior, Office of the Secretary, in Washington, D.C. As I sat at my desk typing, the phone rang. It was my mother calling from her job with the Central Intelligence Agency. Her voice was shaky and tearful as she explained that President John F. Kennedy had been shot while riding in a motorcade in the streets of Dallas, Texas. After a few more moments I hung up and in a stunned voice told my supervisor the startling news. Our whole office sat in disbelief and finally someone turned on a small radio for the latest news reports. Sure enough, the President had been killed by an assassin's bullet. He had died in his wife's arms in a mad rush to Parkland Memorial Hospital in Dallas. The rest of that day was in turmoil in our office and throughout our building—people crying, milling about and discussing the tragedy.

The chain of events and the drama that unfolded in the next few days were unbelievable. Vice President Lyndon Johnson, also in the motorcade, was sworn in as 36th President of the United States on Air Force One as it returned to Washington, bearing the casket of the slain president and his widow. The days that followed revealed that Lee Harvey Oswald was the assassin and as he was being taken from a Dallas jail a man stepped up, shot and killed him. The avenger was Jack Ruby, owner of a Dallas nightclub.

The President's body was returned to the White House to lie instate in the East Room. On Sunday, November 24, the flag draped casket left the White House for its journey to the Capitol. The cortege was escorted by a military honor guard which included a Special Forces member wearing a green beret. (President Kennedy had a special interest in these guerrilla trained troops which he had sent to the jungles of Vietnam). Mrs. Kennedy, in a black suit and black lace mantilla, held the hands of each of her children as she walked behind the casket moving slowly ahead as it finally reached the steps of the Capitol. She and the children moved into place in the rotunda of the Capitol where many eulogies were given. All afternoon and through the night 250,000 people were to file past the coffin in a silent line.

On Monday, November 25, the casket was placed on a caisson drawn by three pairs of matched gray horses—the right row of horses was saddled but riderless. Jacqueline Kennedy, the widow, once again walked behind her husband's casket to St. Matthew's Cathedral for the funeral Mass, accompanied by the slain president's brothers, Attorney General Robert Kennedy and Senator Edward Kennedy.

The caisson bearing the coffin of John F. Kennedy was drawn by three pairs of matched gray horses. The right row of horses was saddled but riderless, following military customs.

After returning to the White House briefly, the funeral procession began its journey to Arlington Cemetery. It took an hour to drive behind the horse drawn caisson as it wound along a three-mile route across the Memorial Bridge. Thousands of people lined the procession route to pay tribute to President Kennedy. The whole nation, as well as foreign countries, was in mourning for the passing of this popular president. Dignitaries from all over the world attended the funeral.

John F. Kennedy was laid to rest in the shadow of the Custis-Lee Mansion on a grassy hill overlooking the Potomac River with the Lincoln Memorial in the distance. An eternal flame at the site marks the grave.

In the words of his favorite song, *"Don't let it be forgot, that once there was a spot, for one brief shining moment, that was known as Camelot."*

Chapter 8

WARS, POLITICS, SOCIETY

Peace cannot be kept by force. It can only be achieved by understanding. — Albert Einstein

Therefore Stand
Eugene Tucker

Uncle Gene came home to Louisville, Kentucky from service in World War II where he was awarded a Bronze Metal for bravery. He was a giant of a man, soft spoken with a trigger sensitive temper that reminded me of Grandma. He had lived in Louisville briefly before being drafted into the US Army and sent overseas. It was not a good idea to make him angry, or to corner him. He recounted an event in the jungle where his unit was ambushed by Japanese soldiers. Hand to hand combat ensued as Japanese soldiers jumped from trees and bushes. He said that he just grabbed a bunch of *"Japs"* and started cutting their throats. He said,

"I must have broken some of their necks with my bare hands".

There was little doubt from those who knew him that he was capable of such feats. He displayed the hooked blade knife that he had used in the melee. I was afraid to touch it. He had suffered a cut down his back, but survival was more urgent than the pain. Like so many veterans he returned to face the same segregation he had left behind. There would be no employment opportunity and no medical assistance to help him and others like him regain some semblance of a "normal" life. Uncle Gene returned home to the Seventh Street Train Station located on the Ohio River waterfront and was ordered to the Negro section of the station. There were two Negro soldiers taken from the station and their eyes plucked out by an angry mob of white men because they refused to go to their section of the station. The outcry over such an unspeakable deed against our soldiers was not heeded and the social order remained.

Uncle Gene stayed around Louisville for a while finding work here and there until he decided to move to Canton, Ohio. I do not know why he chose Canton. I was still in high school at the time and I knew that Canton was not the land of opportunity. The football hall of fame was not there yet. A few years later Mom got the news that Uncle Gene was not doing too well in Canton. She and Uncle Charlie decided that it was time to go get him. About three o'clock one morning Mom, my sister Lorene, my nephew Willie T, and I got into our 1950 Chevrolet and headed to Canton. In the middle of the night we found where he was living and Mom told him we were there to take him home. He was happy to see us and gave Mom no argument. All of Mom's brothers and sisters loved and respected each other. Mom, like Grandma, did not accept no as an answer. We gathered his belongings, placed them into his Ford Crown Victoria and headed back to Louisville with Willie T at the wheel. The caravan returned to Louisville and Uncle Gene would live with Uncle Charlie for a while. Uncle Charlie purchased a van and equipped it with cleaning equipment that he and

Uncle Gene used to service cleaning contracts. This business relationship did not last very long. Uncle Charlie was too demanding.

Uncle Gene moved in with a rather large fair skin woman. He would have difficulty with relationships all his life. The toll of war would haunt him and he retreated into alcohol and drugs. A once proud and vigorous man slowly disintegrated. One day he was found at the rear of a liquor store sitting on a garbage can head bowed as if asleep, but would never awaken again. They said he had died from an overdose of something called "Christmas tree". The images of the violence of war, the loss of hope, and the abandonment by the country he served left him with death as the better alternative to life. We were given the carefully folded American Flag honoring a fallen soldier. I was given his medal of honor and a few handkerchiefs to remember him by.

Charlie, Jr., Uncle Charlie's oldest son, would serve proudly in the US Navy. He saw this as an opportunity to better support his wife and four children. There were three boys and one girl. It was so heartening to see them help and support each other. Their father would come home from his military service and within a few months fall victim to polio. The iron lung, similar to the MRI machine in use today, was used to help patients suffering from polio. The patient was placed in this machine with only the head of the person visible. Oxygen was pumped into the machine to help support breathing. A mirror was positioned for the patient to see who was talking or visiting. He remained in the iron lung for months before life could no longer be supported. His body was returned to Mississippi and placed in a grave covered with briars and weed. I doubt if anyone could locate it now. The children's mother would die later with a rare form of leukemia. The children survived and two of the boys graduated college while taking care of their younger siblings. Their sister would die an untimely death that could be attributed to a "broken heart". The youngest boy continues to struggle to control his life. The boys continue to cling to each other as they pursue their own lives with their families. What a show of courage!

Young men from my community would volunteer for the military or were drafted. They proudly wore the uniforms of the Army, Navy, Marines, and Air Force to attract women both young and old and to show that they were somebody. Younger kids wanted to be like them. Most had joined to experience the world and to gain skills that might help them get better jobs upon their return to civilian life. Many would make a career out of the military. Korea and Viet Nam would be the battlegrounds to beacon them. My friend, Alfonso, returned home from war shell shocked from his duty in the Tank Division. He was afraid to leave the house whenever an airplane flew overhead. He would never recover from his phobia and would never receive any medical assistance from the military. My sister Leona's husband and my cousin Leslie, Jr. became paratroopers out of Fort Campbell Kentucky. They still talk about the thrill of jumping out of planes and the excitement of war. They still support military intervention when there is a world crisis. One of my neighbors and school mate lost his leg. He recalled life at sea on a Navy ship. Another returned home from Viet Nam with a mangled arm due to his effort to save his life by jumping into a barrel of human waste that was being collected for spreading in the rice fields.

Accounts of heroism, bloodshed, victories and death kept coming. I stood in defiance at the draft board as a conscientious objector. I asked myself this question "Is my freedom as important as those for whom my country was asking me to sacrifice my life for?" Treat me with respect and recognize my humanity and I will fight too! My logic was discounted by the draft board and I would struggle with the board until I was thirty five years old. The woman at the draft board had made me her project for life for which I was willing to oblige. I never joined the military.

The Politics of Race
Eugene Tucker

I was about seven years old, when our family lived on Kirby Street in Louisville, Kentucky. Kirby was a short street in the West end of the city where clusters of Negroes lived. We lived next door to a family who were well off by most standards. The father was a dentist and their children were away in college. I don't remember ever seeing them or hearing them speak to my parents. Our little shot gun house had four rooms including a kitchen. We had an outhouse as our toilet. Our water hydrant was outside near our side door. This hydrant was a source of grave concern during the winter. Water often froze during the winter, so it was urgent that rags be wrapped around the pipes and sometimes warmed with boiling water from our kitchen. If we left a tiny drip from the faucet a long icicle would form, but the water in the faucet would not freeze. One could barely see our house for the tall vegetation that separated our house from our neighbors. This vegetation also covered the front of our house. We had a small front, rear and side yards. The outside of our house always seemed moist and dreary with a lot of moss. We had moved here from Tie Plant, where we had lived upon our arrival in Louisville a few years earlier.

Each day when my sister and I came home from school, we walked down Kirby Street through the white neighborhood with paved streets, sidewalks, and green manicured lawns. The paving and sidewalks stopped abruptly when we entered the Negro portion of Kirby Street. We had gravel and dirt roads without sidewalks. Some of our neighbors' yards had grass. Others were bare dirt. The houses were a lot nicer than those in Tie Plant. Most people hung their wash outside to dry on long clothes lines. I noticed with wonderment as I walked home about the transition from sidewalks to gravel. City water and sewer were available to these houses along our route. Only city water was available in our neighborhood. Some people had placed water on the inside of their houses, but there was no sewer service for inside plumbing, so the outhouse was our only means. It was here in this neighborhood that I began to understand the meaning of the word *"politics"*. Our section of the city was known as *"Little Africa"*. I later learned that in every section of the city where Negroes lived, descriptive names were given such as Smoke Town, The East End, and Newberg. In every case paved roads, sidewalks, and sewers stopped at the edge of each compound. Each of these enclaves was communities within themselves, with bitter rivalries established between them. I noticed that at every local or statewide political election a coat of black tar would be spread over our gravel and dirt roads. I asked my mother "why was that tar put down on our roads"? She answered:

"Those old politicians are trying to do something nice for us so we would vote for them."

The Negro woman who was a precinct worker went door-to-door making sure you voted Democrat. No other party was ever mentioned, but it was known by everyone in our neighborhood that a vote for Democrats would mean you could continue working for the sanitation department, and get the cleaning jobs down at city hall and other government offices. People were driven to the polls and escorted into the voting booths to cast their ballots for the chosen candidate. Every year and on every election the process was the same. I grew up believing that there was only one party that had any interest in the plight of the Negro. I had forgotten that President Lincoln, a Republican, had freed the slaves and that his plans for the freed slaves had been dashed after he was assassinated.

The tar would follow us to every neighborhood in which we lived through my high school years. Mom never appreciated the tar. It kept our floors dirty and sticky. It was easier to remove the mud from the floors after the rains. The tar required extra effort and a different cleaner for our linoleum floors. I do not remember anyone being satisfied with the tar, but the politicians continued the practice and demanded our vote. As I grew older I began to question the practice and wondered "who were these people making these decisions"? I remember reading the story about "tar baby" in elementary school. Perhaps, this was a reminder for us not to forget who we were. The books we used in school were those discarded by the white schools. We had only one public high school for the entire city of Louisville, Kentucky and the surrounding counties. So, Negro children had to be bussed in from the counties to attend high school. There would be conflicts from overcrowding and the usual community rivalry. I became a very silent revolutionary without realizing I had become such until many years later.

Today it stresses me to see politicians, most of whom are White Democrats, showing up at predominantly Negro churches and being warmly embraced and sins and transgressions unconditionally forgiven. They sit in the warm and safe confines of the church followed by the ever present press and forecast their plans to deal with the plight of Black citizens. They leave to declare a separation between church and state, while repeating the same issues that began during reconstruction. But, solutions never come. Is this the politics of the new age? When will the Negro understand the game and how to play it? Does anyone remember who lost the civil war and the work of the Democrats of the south to disenfranchise the Negro during and after reconstruction? Does anyone remember who was behind the Black Codes and the KKK and the ouster of the Negro from the political process and the right to vote? Does anyone remember the role the Ex Slave played in the rebuilding of our nation immediately after the Civil

War and the role southern Democrats played to reduce them to a different form of slavery and to marginalize a race for over one hundred years? The vote of Black America should matter and not be taken for granted. Perhaps, it is time for a Black American to step forward into the political arena with credentials to be seriously considered for the Presidency of the United States and above all supported by his race. Political party affiliation is an unfortunate avenue to the White House. Command of issues, personal values, world vision, and a clear and comprehensive plan should comprise the portfolio of the one seeking such a high office to lead the world we live in. I believe such persons reside in this land. Let them come forth without the fear of reprisals and the venom that haunts those brave enough to try today. For a great nation to survive, do we deserve as much?

THE BIG PUT DOWN
Harriet Burgess

Politics were never a big issue in our family. There were discussions but not as an everyday thing. One exception might have been my Grandfather McWhorter. As a child living on the farm, Granddaddy used to fight the Civil War often at the Sunday dinner table when all the city relatives were home for a visit. He was a 'dyed in the wool' Southerner and fought the 'damn Yankees' regularly. Probably those feelings dated back to when his father was a doctor with the South and operated on many wounded Confederate soldiers around the Fairfax area.

Through the years growing up I heard him many times refer to the 'dam Black Republicans'. It meant nothing to me until one day, years later, after I had left the farm and moved to Arlington, Virginia to live with my mother and new stepfather. I was riding with my best friend Chloe in the back seat of their family car. Her mom and dad were up front and their conversation turned to politics. I naively leaned forward and said:

"Mr. Wherry, are you a Black Republican?"

He turned red in the face and the shouted answer was:

"You don't know what you're talking about missy!"

I haven't had much interest in politics since.

Letters to Frank
Keith Severin

April 21, 2005

Dear Frank, you're gooder'n a pot of gold!! For sure, you certainly took good care of me the night of April 12th, Tuesday a week ago. I was in the hospital that night after surgery on my shoulder and I had a folder of wonderful reading material that had come from you the day before. I had a good, comfortable bed and it was quiet, and I had a wonderful reading light. I didn't feel a lot like sleeping, so I read everything you sent. Much of it, the opera stuff, was enjoyed by me first and then passed on to Barbara (my wife). All that material came, of course, after your letter. More about that later.

Since I wrote to Peggy and Bob today bringing them up to date on my doings this past 10 days or so, I am enclosing a copy of that for you.

As you will see/read, I've been back in the hospital this week. While it just now occurs to me that I didn't mention it *per se* to Peggy, it seems that reason for this last hospitalization was concluded to be vertigo. Okay, but no one knows for sure what causes vertigo. The most "prominent" reason is a viral infection in the inner ear. Okay, but---?

Your second letter and package made me envious – all the swimming you do, the extent of it – 26 laps. Great, and your bicycling too. These are things you do to move your body. Horseback, the horse does it. Little motion on my part, no real exercise, in my opinion.

I was amused at your fellow attendees vs. what you thought of it. As I've said, it's really just the "what" to most everyone. Hardly ever the "how" and almost never the "why". In other words, it's just the "what" never the "so what?"

This sort of fits into the conversation I had late the other night with a young orderly in the hospital, an Iranian 35 years old, here with a green card and studying nursing. A good, sharp fellow, well spoken and very thoughtful. Odam, the name of the fellow, says fundamentalism is the real problem in Iran and most of the Middle East, and that's what concerns him about the new Pope. Odam and I talked about competition, and capitalism and materialism too. He's set on the US, it's the overall best there is, and if you work you can have as much of it as you want. Odam is proud of his green card and said that now he's worth something, that if he were in Iran now and something happened to him the US would sit up and take notice. When he was still a youngster back in Iran during the Iran-Iraq war and the bombing was taking place and he and his brother and sister clung to their mother's skirts during the bombing, no one would have noticed at all if something had happened to him. He was nothing. Quite a story and belief.

You may find it interesting, but I asked Odam about "change", and we spoke about it. Remember, I spoke to your classes there at the university about change, different kinds of change and how we look for changes and how we might prepare ourselves for change. Certainly lots of change is going on now. Just look at the Vatican, and don't overlook the US House Ethics Committee and Mr. Delay. There's Mr. Bolton, too. Whew!! Lots to read. I say again, I do really wish I were a good reader and could read fast. Barbara and Kenneth and Peggy are fantastic readers.

You write that academia was the good place to be. Okay, I certainly wouldn't disagree, but where ever one is there must be the opportunity to observe and think and question about things. If there's a rut, it must be a wide one and not so deep that the stars can't be seen, and certainly not be a short one where you're not far from the end.

More again on sausage gravy, maybe I can explain it this time. From what you write, I think you assume that "sausage" means link sausage, sausage done up kind of like wieners. Yes, there is link sausage, but there is also bulk sausage, pork that is ground up, not "packaged" that looks like ground beef/hamburger. It is that, bulk sausage, which is used to make sausage gravy. Fry, or brown small chunks of the bulk sausage in a skillet, then add your flour, while stirring, then add milk slowly and continue to stir. You should end up with gravy with bits of sausage in it – no flour dumplings if you have stirred it diligently. That's the latest version of sausage gravy – and I sure could have used some for breakfast, or any time, while I was in the hospital. For one meal I had a good looking biscuit on my tray, but nothing to go with it except a wish for it to be there along with sausage gravy or some good jam, not even any butter required.

I'm glad you liked the magazine *Reminiscences* that I sent. I forgot to make note of an article in it - "I'm curious about this antique". In the article, on the left edge of the left hand page, a picture of something someone had found while hunting in South Dakota and didn't know what it is. It looks like a long corkscrew with a couple of loops twisted in toward one end. What that is, is a fence post, one that is just screwed into the ground and the fence wire run through the loops from one post to another. It is for temporary fencing, a forerunner to electric fencing, certainly a forerunner to electric fencing powered by battery or solar panel. If you still have that magazine and can find the article, please send it along and I will respond to the query.

April 24th

I had thought I would get the above into the mail the other day, but…so, here are more—more thoughts and things that have occurred to me since then. Many of them were provoked by the things you have sent recently, and that's quite a batch of many good things.

First, however is to say that this morning I told Barbara that it seems everyday now I am able to use my arm a bit more, raise it more. Tomorrow I will finally see the doctor about the arm and get more definitive about it. Likely there will be physical therapy, and that I can use. It has been prescribed for the dizziness (vertigo), that's for the head. I need some for the arm, in all likelihood, and I am to the point that I need some for my back too. The lower back is gone, vertebrae have fused and more are beginning, and there's a spur there too. That was quite obvious in an x-ray Dr. Snyder took about a month ago. I guess all that comes from the milk – whole milk and buttermilk – I like so much and have drunk so much of over the years. I recall drinking milk straight from the cow, trying to get the squirt of milk from the teat aimed into my mouth, not getting all over my face before finally getting it right. Warm goat's milk is okay too, but not after it has been cooled. Then of course, and coming from what I am and was for so long, there's kumiss, fermented mares milk, that I got well acquainted with in Soviet Central Asia and Bashkir. It has about a 6% alcohol content.

One more thing before going on to recent thoughts. The other night in the hospital, when I was self-administering morphine, I spoke to the nurse about painkillers and what the feeling is to come out from their effects. She agreed that today's painkillers are good, but ever so much better than in the days of ether. Ether! Ether! that brought back memories – and you might say that the other night I was definitely in a state of memories – never, never land, only these memories are true, really happened, even though they took place in Samoa, a near-paradise land to many.

Dave Butchart, my boss in Samoa, had a 6 cylinder Chrysler inboard motor in his boat, a 20-24 foot boat, the biggest one in Samoa with the exception of the 50 foot Navy long boats that were used to supply the outlying villages that were totally inaccessible by road. Ruthie, Dave's wife, was the chief nurse at the hospital. Dave didn't use his boat all that much, didn't start it very often, and it was usually a job to get it started there in the humid tropics. *Voila!* a can of ether from the hospital usually did the trick. Take out a couple of spark plugs, pour in a bit, just a bit of ether, put the plugs back, and vroom! The engine almost always started right up. If not, at least the combustion chambers got dried out. Yes, a use of ether in Samoa. Dave was a smart and pretty practical fellow, definitely knew about volatile things – could and did make real martini, only gin and a bit of vermouth. No ice!

Thinking of Dave's boat and how we got it started brings back another memory of about the same genre, something that Barbara wasn't too happy about with me – again in Samoa. I was out in the bush with a couple of my Samoan helpers and we needed to start a fire. I didn't smoke, had no matches, and certainly the Samoans didn't have any in their lava lavas. (If they were in the village and needed a light, a youngster would bring them a hot cinder from one of the always going fires. Actually, few of the Samoans smoked.) So, there we were, Paka Maae, Alofa, and a couple of other Samoans and I in need of something to start a fire. There we were in the bush, we and the jeep pickup that I had to drive. Using my head and thinking about things, I had an idea. Yes, I had a crescent wrench in the truck. With it I loosened the fuel line to the carburetor and soaked a bit of rag with the gasoline that came out. Paka moved away from the truck with the rag and went to find a long stick that I asked him to find while I put the fuel line back together. Then, I loosened one spark plug wire, raised it up, getting it as far from the engine block as I could. I told Paka to hold the stick so the rag was close to the end of the spark plug wire. Then, I got into the truck turned on the key and hit the starter once, just once was all I wanted, so I did it myself. Guess what?? On the end of that stick we had something would/could start our fire with!! The Samoans were amazed at Sevelini's ability to get fire without matches. When I told Barbara about all this, she wasn't pleased, thinking about what the Samoans might do, be less careful, etc. Any way, just another memory.

One more about ether in Samoa. There was a lady who was quite important in one of the villages who had a problem. Her dog, a male, was always running off, getting into trouble when any of the female dogs in the village came into season. Clearly, he should be neutered. She asked me could I do it, she having heard about some of the things I had done with the cattle at the dairy. Sure, why not?? I had castrated pigs, and it shouldn't be much different to cut a dog.

So, I asked Ruthie, the source of supply for needed things, for a can of ether. I got one of my fellows to go with me and we went to the village. The lady got her dog, my "assistant" held him while I made a mask (rolled paper into a cone and put cotton into it) and put it over the dog's face. Poured in some ether, don't ask how much, but it was enough, and I proceeded to change that dog's physiology. It worked. Sure glad ether was available. Ruthie was a good Samaritan.

One other time I recall when the hospital in Samoa was the source of needed supplies. A cow at the dairy was down with milk fever, she just having calved and had low blood glucose. (It was only a couple of semesters ago at Davis that I had a course in basic, very preliminary veterinary medicine, and I remembered about milk fever, that it was treated with calcium glucose.) So, off I go to the hospital to get some calcium glucose. Yes, there is some but only in the size doses used for humans. Okay, give me about 10 of those bottles and a couple of syringes. Off I go back to the dairy, about 8 miles or so on coral roads, through the valley to the dairy. The cow is still down, so I stick her in the neck with a needle and inject a bottle of calcium glucose. Being efficient, I leave the needle in place- just as is done today – and keep using it as more bottles of calcium glucose are injected. I used all I had, and pretty quick the old cow was up on her feet and going on. Enele, the dairy manager, and his wife, were surprised to see all that and were pleased to have the cow up and going, since she was one of the best ones. Whew! again, more or less by the seat of the pants, trying to remember what I could and doing what might work, and it did work.

Here's the last of the war stories, this one taking place in the autumn of 1950 at Dixon, when I was doing practice teaching of voc-ag at Dixon High School, near Davis. Glenn Caldwell was my master teacher, a very good man, very practical, and one who gave free rein so long as he felt confidence in you. (I remember Elmer Jones was one of the students. Elmer, a good, very big fellow, much bigger than I- not yet 21 years old. Elmer would see me walking toward him, he would just hold an arm out to the side, and I would walk under. Then, we would both turn around and look at one another, he giving me a big grin.) Anyway, it came time to teach the students, all boys and members of the Future Farmers of America, about castrating pigs as part of the swine husbandry we were studying. Needed to do it, show them how. As it happened, Richard Caldwell, one of Glenn's sons, had a litter of pigs just the right age and size that needed to be castrated. So, off we go and Glenn told me to do the first pig, show the boys how it's done. "Keith, you've castrated pigs before, haven't you?" "No, but I've seen it done and know what you have to do." Whew! Glenn had enough confidence to let me go ahead and work on one of his son's pigs.

Wouldn't you know it? The pig caught for me to castrate had only one testicle outside of its body, a cryptorchid. I removed the one testicle showing and certainly couldn't find another, probably looked pretty puzzled. Glen, standing and watching closely, didn't know what to think, but checked for himself and was satisfied that my "procedure and diagnosis" were correct. From there on, things went smoothly, the students learning to castrate pigs and to work with what they had. The pigs in Richard's litter grew normally. Do the best you can with what you have and go on.

Now, back to you (Frank) and what you've prompted.

Glad your little bird was ready to be picked up 10 days ago, and I hope you got that done. Yes, it makes sense for you to have company, since you've not been up in her for so long.

You see why we like the Tremont in Chicago. It fits in all regards and is well located. Good folks there, and John, the head man concierge, I guess, knows us.

Marcel continues to impress- a solid young man, a solid family and getting a solid practical- hands on- education from the bank. I'm sure he will go far. Brandon, my young friend here will graduate from high school soon. He's going to Christopher Newport here in Newport News, Virginia, not far from us. Five thousand students and with much hands on, including by the President, Mr. Trible, a former US Senator from Virginia.

The 26 pages of "What I heard about Iraq" says a lot, says it over and over, and certainly draws a picture of us and ours, and what we are. Sad… I agree, sourcing would give it more credence. The picture drawn is pretty bleak, not at all pretty.

As you can tell, I've been pretty much laid up for the past time, so have gotten some reading done, much of it from you. How much I enjoy – and certainly Barbara too – the material on opera. We also receive a lot on opera from the NYT from Cynthia Enloe. She's another one who stays busy, on the road, on the speaking trail and writing as well as keeping her classes at Clark going.

I guess I find it no surprise that you are getting your book *Jean De Florette from Anchorage*. I guess one could say that the internet does facilitate Marketing, if the definition of a market is where buyer and seller come together. What's the interest in the De Florette book?

Also, thanks for all the articles about George Kennan, the statements made at his memorial service. I've learned much more about him, and to have the statement by Gorbachev from Kennan is particularly good, since as I've told you, they (those two men) are my men of the 20th century. I was particularly struck by one statement attributed by Kennan. It comes from his book, *Sketches from Life,* apparently written after he had traveled across Russia/Siberia on board a train. The statement, as in Blair Ruble's statement goes:

"…Kennan struggled with how best to understand the dignified beauty of such a 'gifted, appealing people' whose lives are set against a landscape that should drive one to despair." 'The answer is anybody's,' he answered himself. 'But I, for my part, should have thought with the sights and sounds of Siberia still vivid in my mind, that in these circumstances it would be wisest to try neither to help nor to harm… and to leave the Russian people – encumbered neither by foreign sentimentality nor foreign antagonism – to work out their destiny in their own peculiar way.'"

That statement reminds me of what I used to say when I was asked when the Soviet Union would change. My response was, "When some yet-to-be-born Russian comes along." I said that before Gorbachev came in 1985, and even after he came along with glasnost and perestroika there were changes, changes for sure, many of them material changes, but changes nonetheless. Of course, what does "change" mean? The surface was being scratched.

I've been told by Russians that Gorbachev really was not liked very much in the USSR, probably so, and very likely he was more highly regarded in the West – say by Mrs. Thatcher- but in any case the surface was being scratched. Underlying that surface, though, is still the Russian soul, and that soul is very deep out in the countryside. Maybe a globalization/"modernization" takes more hold in urban places and as the countryside, the peasantry, is increasingly less, more of the old folks die off, there's less family back in the country, that aspect of Russian life more and more diluted, the "Russian soul factor" will be less important.

Another bit in the Ruble statement where he describes a meeting between Gorbachev and Kennan is good, and it brings memories to me. That statement goes *"Mikhail Gorbachev perhaps best captured this special relationship between Kennan and Russia when he told Professor Kennan, 'We in our country believe that a man may be the friend of another country and remain, at the same time, a loyal devoted citizen of his own; and that is the way we view you.'"*

Just about now, late, very late April 1964, I was with two other officers of the embassy in Rostov, there on a Sunday morning with a flat tire on our Ford station wagon. We had been in that part of the USSR on a road trip and wanted/had to be back in Moscow before May 1st. Anyway, the other fellows took the flat tire and went off trying to find a place to get it fixed. I stayed with the car, it "parked" close to a collective farm market, which was really busy that Sunday morning. Not many non-Soviet vehicles on the road those days, so that Ford station wagon attracted attention. A fellow came along, looked at the car, and we started talking, I picking up on the fact that he was carrying a bundle of tomato plants, it being planting time. I asked about his tomato plants and told him that I was from California and had grown about a hectare (2.5 acres) of tomatoes in the summer to earn money to attend the university where I studied agriculture. "From California?" Yes. Do you know Fresno? Lots of Armenians there and I am Armenian." Yes, I know Fresno. I used to drive through that place on the way to the university.

Quite a few people were gathering around listening and looking. How long have you been in our country? What do you think of our country? It's quite interesting, very interesting to travel in and see things and meet people, etc. Then, came the cruncher — always a flag waver in the crowd. "So you have been in our country more than 1 ½ years and you like it. Tell me, which do you like better, your country or our country?" (That's an exact quote- never to be forgotten!!!) Swallow hard, Severin, you're supposed to be a diplomat, at least you work at the embassy, what do you say??

Thank goodness for tomatoes! The Armenian with the tomato plants spoke right up. "What a dumb question. Of course, every man loves his own country better than any other." That did it. I shook the man's hand and said I hoped one day he would visit his friends in Fresno. See why Gorbachev's statement about Kennan struck a note??

The piece you sent by the Australian correspondent, Chris Clark, who went back to Moscow after having been gone 10 years, since 1995, was ok not more, at least in my opinion. You wrote that you'd like to see a description of the changes 1989 to date.

Nothing Clark wrote is any surprise to me, no surprise, only disappointing in what has happened there. So sad, and there I go back to what I used to say/think when I would hear a Russian/Soviet say they wanted to be like America. They were looking forward to the "dollarization" of their money. To me, that said they really, really did not know us. Sad, sad, sad!!

I will send the Clark piece to Kenneth (my son) and see if I get any response from him. Don't forget, he spent nearly 2 years there, going to school and playing with Soviet youngsters and going around with me on Wednesday afternoons and Saturdays and Sundays seeing how they lived, what they bought, how they did things. And Kenneth is an excellent observer and gets on with people very well and very quickly. I look forward to his response. Will let you know.

What should I say, given what I've just said? "Who's to blame, or who gets the credit?"

Of the several statements about Mr. Kennan that you sent, and thanks again for doing that, I think the one by Anders Stephanson, Associate Professor of History at Columbia, was quite good, perhaps, a bit more comprehensive in its own way.

Frank, this plenty, more than plenty for one session of you soaking up sunshine there on your sofa. You can tell I've had some time to do things other than getting things done outside. I do miss the out of doors activity. That's for sure – and probably the reason I have little appetite these days. Barbara is good, asking what I'd like and doing even more special things in her kitchen. As I tell her, and told the nurses in the hospital, I am spoiled. I recognize it, admit it and like it - and am thankful for and to those who spoil me.

So, take care, the best kind of care of yourself.

Chapter 9

RELATIONSHIPS

Only a life lived for others, is a life worth while.
Albert Einstein

WAS THERE A COLOR BARRIER?
Harriet Burgess

In the late 1800s on the family farm at Leeton in Chantilly, Virginia, there lived a black man named Buck Brooks. He was well over six feet tall and very strong. He was born at Leeton and lived in a small cabin in the woods adjoining our farm. He never married and all his life was spent working there.

I don't know much about his life, only casual comments from time to time made by my grandparents as I was growing up. Apparently he was regarded with respect and affection—virtually treated as a member of the family. He ate all his meals with the family, prepared by spinster Great Aunt Harriotte. Often, I recall my grandmother telling stories of Buck and how devoted he was to them all.

Buck (standing), fishing with a friend on the Potomac River

His life was one of hard work, putting in crops with a team of mules and harvest time was shared with other workers from nearby farms. His favorite pastime was fishing and often he could be seen putting a line in the Potomac River, a short journey from the farm. He came home many times proudly displaying his 'good catch' which he shared with the family. He had friends and some family and I suppose on Sundays he did his visiting as well as fishing.

Buck was often sent to Fairfax Courthouse in the horse and buggy to meet the train from Washington, D.C. which carried my great-grandfather Turberville home on weekends after working at the Patent Office during the week. Sometimes the train was late but Buck patiently waited for the old man. It was about a 20-mile round trip back to Leeton pulled by the family horse named Lord Fairfax.

Buck was a part of the joys and sorrows of the family as the years went by. He lived at Leeton to a "ripe old age" and was sorely missed when he died. He was buried in the family cemetery there on the farm.

There was a family of Brooks living up the road when I was young. I guess they were related in some way to Buck. The head of that family was a carpenter and in the 1920s he helped to build my grandparent's house across the field from Leeton.

"Yes'um"
Eugene Tucker

I became aware of the relationship between the races at the age of five. My baby sister, Leona, and I would wonder around the corner to the little neighborhood store in Grenada, Mississippi to spend our pennies. The store owner had a mentally retarded son who meandered through the store scaring people with the strange sounds he made. To our surprise the boy, who was about fifteen years old, demanded that we call him "Mister". Mom told us this was the way things were here and that people including children had been killed for disobeying the rules. Leona and I did not understand. We had been told that we greeted adults with this courtesy. We observed adults addressing White people with "Yes'um", "No Sir", and "No Mam", with our heads slightly bowed in seeming reverence. When we moved to Louisville, Kentucky in the 1940's, we noticed Negroes addressing White people by their first names without fear of reprisals. They even looked each other in the eye. We were warned again not to take this freedom of speech back to Granada, Mississippi. This warning would be clearly understood when the world saw that a fifteen year old boy from Chicago, Illinois had been lynched in a little town called Lucky, Mississippi for allegedly whistling at a White woman in 1954. This would touch off demonstrations and racial tensions never before seen in this country. Boycotts and forms of civil disobedience would spread both north and south.

I experienced many social changes during my early years. Throughout my elementary and secondary school years I attended segregated schools. There was no such thing as separate but equal, just separate. In our "Little Africa" neighborhood, the title given to our community, there were a few white families. One family lived three houses up from us on 37th and Young Street in Louisville, Kentucky. They attended their all White schools; we attended our all Black schools. We rode the city buses or walked to get to school passing their schools along the way. This was the way it had always been and we heard little discussion about changing the situation until 1954 Civil Rights Act was passed. Our neighborhood disintegrated. There was both "Black" and "White" flight. Shawnee High School, an all White high school, closed and never reopened. The White neighbors sold their houses to Blacks and moved to the suburbs. This beautiful school remained in ruin for years while the city struggled with its future.

A White friend of my Dad sold his house to us when he decided to move to the Highlands, a wealthy White section on the outskirts of the city. My old neighborhood imploded. All of our churches were displaced. Some moved to occupied White churches while others struggled to relocate to newly constructed sites. Some would fail from their debt burden, others would flourish. Chaos abounded while the city fathers scratched their heads. They tried constructing public housing in the area where we lived which turned into a disaster and later abandoned. Grass and weeds engulfed the land where our house once stood, the baseball field, the abandoned churches and the land where the houses of our friends and neighbors both Black and White. The city plans for redeveloping the old community where I grew up has taken some forty years to be implemented. In the meantime Negroes began to relocate into all areas of the city. There were several cross burnings by the KKK, houses bombed, and physical assaults throughout the city. Relative calm grips the city today. A recent Harvard University study on the status of school desegregation covering the period 1954 through 2001 was released on January 18, 2004 and reported in the Washington Post newspaper. The report concluded that the states of Kentucky and Washington maintain the highest level of school integration in the nation with New York and Illinois the most segregated for Black Americans. However, the overall trend for Black Americans and Latinos was down almost reaching the level of 1969 when Dr. Martin Luther King, Jr. was killed. It is feared that the rate of "resegregation" might reach that of 1954 if the trend continues. Changing demographics was cited as one explanation.

As a child I was never told by my family or neighbors that my color made me inferior. My family was too busy trying to survive and protect their children from the negative influences that surrounded us each day. Protecting us often meant keeping us from the restricted water fountains or the public parks down on the river front. My parents got along well with their White friends, some of whom were their employers. One of Dad's friends even willed me a set of books that had been commissioned by the US Congress that contained the writing of the presidents through 1940. Only 1,000 sets were produced and I am the owner of one of those sets. Some restoration is now needed. Mom became friends with one of the owners of the Fall City Brewery. Mom worked for her one day a week. Mom said they often visited when she was supposed to work and would often go out together to look for antiques. My aunt Lucille, who lived in Mississippi, put together one of the most elaborate antique collections in the region with the help of her White friends for whom she had worked. Most of the men and women with whom I worked seemed "color blind." I would feel the strain of color in public places on many occasions, once being asked to leave a Chinese restaurant in Suitland, Maryland in 1960.

I was fortunate to travel throughout the continental United States beginning in the 1950's. I experienced the rear of the bus, denial at food counters, ordered from restaurants, denied housing, and even employment opportunities. These encounters with prejudice did not alter my belief in the goodness of man or in my determination to be free. I was not to be denied, for the world was far too large for me to sit and drown in self pity, or to wait for someone to give me freedom. I realized how blessed I was that God had given me exceptional talent, an inherited strong will from my ancestors, and a quiet yet determined desire to succeed. To the credit of my ancestors, parents, and community, my family harbored no hate or resentment for our situation in life. A little difficulty builds character, my Grandpa would say as he bounced me on his knee while reciting lines from the "Village Blacksmith".

I recall an occasion when one of my colleagues who was in graduate school at George Washington University and was having difficulty with an assignment in mathematical statistics. I asked if I could look at the problem. As he handed me the book, he said *"I don't think you would understand this."* Within a few moments I gave him the answer. Whereupon, he asked me how did I know that? I said to him, politely, that I could solve every problem in his book. He never approached me again.

TOGETHERNESS
Thelma Webb Wright

School life began in Montclair, New Jersey. A town of mansions, millionaires and chauffeured limousines and live in servants. The wealthy sent their children to private schools and the children of the colored servants went to the public schools, as did I.

My class photo of 1930 counts seven white pupils and eight colored. Being in the minority group meant nothing to me. Why should it? I knew nothing of the segregation in our country.

By third grade we moved from wealthy Montclair to the small town of Cedar Grove where there were no servants, thus no colored children in my class. Again, this made no impression on me. Why should it?

My mother became quite ill during this time and Dad hired a colored woman, probably from Montclair, to live with us, prepare meals, and do the chores required to keep a home going.

One day, I overheard a conversation between my mother and the colored lady.

Mother, a born southerner, who was raised in North Carolina asked, *"Do you like living in the north, or would you rather live in the south?"*

She said, *"I'd rather live in the south. I know how far I can go there."*

Her answer seemed to please my mother but puzzled me. What did she mean about how far she could go?

At seventeen we moved to Williamsburg, Virginia. My first exposure to segregation happened when I was riding my bike to Matthew Whaley High School. I passed a large brick school built especially for colored students. The term used was, "equal but separate."

Living in Williamsburg soon educated me on the definition of segregation. The local train station had two water fountains with a sign, "colored" over one and "white" over the second fountain. Lavatory doors had signs "colored" and "white". Colored were never seen at the one movie theater or in restaurants. I thought, "This is what the colored lady who was helping mother in New Jersey meant when she said, 'I know how far I can go'."

This new way of life didn't really bother me. Why should it? I was busy in the "white" world of teenagers. And teenagers are in a world of their own!

World War 11 abruptly forced my teen age life into the real world. Some of my senior classmates joined the service. This was real, frightening and would they come back alive? Some did not.

War does not stop romance, probably it hastens the need to fulfill what females of my generation were taught... our main job in life was to marry, raise a family and make a good home for a husband. If we didn't marry we did have three career choices... teacher, nurse or secretary. Period! The thought of blood made me throw up, so nursing was not a choice for me. My poor spelling and having to learn short hand eliminated any hope of becoming a secretary. To be a teacher one had to have four years of college. Cost and the thought of four more years of school cancelled that option in a hurry.

I was saved by falling in love and choosing marriage to John William Wright. We moved to the big city of Richmond which opened many opportunities to further my education in a subject I knew little about...segregation.

I was able to find a job at Miller and Rhodes department store in the photographic department. It was interesting with the challenge of selling photos to customer's who believed they didn't look like THAT and wanted another set of proofs. Diplomatically assuring them the double chins, bags under the eyes and wrinkles would not show in the final photo sometimes helped.

I rode the public bus to and from work taking whatever seat was available. Often it was in the back. One day John came home from work very upset, *"One of the girls in my office saw you sitting in the back of the bus. In the south the colored sit in the back. From now on you sit in the front or stand in the front."*

My response came fast. *"My New Jersey second grade class picture has more colored kids than white kids. We played together, ate together and sat next to each other and it didn't hurt any of us."*

My mother-in-law joined her son in battle, *"In the south you do as your husband says and DO NOT show anybody your class picture."*

I did not exhibit my class picture, however, I continued to sit on any vacant seat available, be it in the front, middle or back. To add to the scene, I never sat next to a colored person without first asking if they minded. That opened interesting conversations. One young lady nodded permission and said, *"We can clean their house, cook for them, and take care of their kids, but we aren't good enough to sit in the front of the bus."*

I was maturing into a Yankee who refused to accept southern tradition. That was 1943.

In the spring of 1944, John received the dreaded letter from Uncle Sam that began with the word, "Greetings". A date, time and place for induction into the Army followed the salutation. He left for army training and I left for New Jersey to await our expected baby and where my long time friends lived and where there would be no segregation.

In the summer of 1945 the war was over. John returned to his job in Richmond and I followed with our baby daughter. We moved into a little bungalow bought on the G.I. bill for $8,000. The war did not change segregation in the south. It still existed strong as ever and the colored knew how far they could go.

By the time I had my fourth baby, I also had a wonderful colored girl named, Virginia, who came once a week to preserve my sanity. We became friends and shared the many necessary chores to keep the house in order. I was so appreciative of Virginia I gave her a raise. When the couple on the street whom she also worked for heard about it from

Virginia, the irate wife came to visit me with a lecture of how I was spoiling Virginia and causing trouble. My reaction was to increase Virginia's raise by another dollar.

A young friend with two little girls wanted Virginia to help her one day a week. Virginia agreed to this. After working a couple of weeks at the new job, I sensed something was not right. When I'd question Virginia, she shrugged her shoulders and said nothing in words until I demanded to know what was going on. Instead of paying Virginia money, the woman handed her clothes her little girls could no longer wear. That was her payment! This Yankee was livid and made a phone call that ended Virginia's job and also a friendship with me. I learned that this was not an unusual way to "pay" the colored.

It has been a struggle of many years but life has changed for the colored, which means life has also changed for the white. I am grateful and happy to see the positive changes. I appreciate what my second grade class taught me... we played together, ate together and sat next to each other and it didn't hurt any of us.

(note: The term "colored" was proper during this period of our history. The term "black" came much later.)

Who Wears The Pants
Eugene Tucker

Women are the weaker sex was the term I grew up hearing as a young man. I often wondered what this meant. Were women physically weaker or perhaps mentally weaker than men? I had a mother, three sisters, a host of aunts, cousins, grandparents and a great grandmother who played significant roles in my life. Grandma, her mother and her grandmother survived the cotton fields of slavery working along side men in addition to bearing children and performing domestic chores. Aunt Rena lifted a five hundred pound bell to be placed in the bell tower of her church while the men stood around trying to determine who was able to lift the bell. Grandma often said "I can outwork any man!" I watched my mother work from sun up to sun down each and every day without seeming to tire. These women did not enjoy the privilege of being placed on pedestals, or pampered with exotic fragrances, flowers, and chocolates. They did not have housekeepers and nannies to lessen their burden. There was little doubt in the mind of this young boy that the females around me could stand toe to toe with any man. These early impressions of women have remained with me throughout my life. They gave me no reason to think of them as the "weaker sex". These women also survived their mates.

I felt that I could survive a whipping from my Dad. I had no such confidence with my mother. A look from her was sufficient until I discovered several years later that death was not eminent, if I misbehaved. Grandma would confront her teenage children, who were larger and seemingly stronger, without any hesitation. She would say as she stood in their faces with a pair of brass knuckles hidden on her hand:

> *"You don't back talk me!"*
> *"I gave birth to you, and I will kill and call you!"*

Her children did not choose to pursue the matter and retreated in silence, sometime murmuring under their breath. I was always careful not to upset Grandma. I had seen her in action. Her sometime gentle manner could be quite deceptive. When Grandma became old she continued to live alone. She kept a large bolo knife at the head of her bed and a pistol under her pillow. When asked if she was afraid to be along at the age of one hundred, she would say

> *"Somebody can break in on me if they want to. They ain't goin to walk out of here!"*

During the days of slavery and the reconstruction period that followed it was more likely that women would survive a dispute with their white masters than a Negro male. After all women could satisfy other pleasures of their masters. Grandma maintained all financial records when she and Grandpa were sharecroppers and would confront the landowner at the end of the year when their records did not agree. She was determined not to be cheated while Grandpa was reluctant to stand firm for fear of retribution. They were able to accumulate a small fortune, owning two Model T cars, horses, cows, and a farm. Grandma was in control. This Ashanti trait was passed along to her off springs. They all learned to plan, manage, save, adapt to changing circumstances and succeed. One of her daughters formed her own successful beauty care business. Another became a collector of antiques with a collection that would rival any well off collector. My mother was the chief financial officer in our house and managed all the affairs. I marvel at her ability to stretch our meager resources to keep us fed, clothed, and sheltered. Most of Grandma's eleven children would own their homes. None thought of themselves as being inferior. They accepted the challenge of life and used it to inspire themselves and their children and their relatives including me. I was fortunate to grow up observing the strength of women in a truly shared relationship where each understood and accepted the role each could best play. Gender does not determine who wears the pants.

It's a Son!
Keith Severin

Today, March 7th, is a special day – Kenneth's 50th birthday, so, of course, lots of memories. Ken was born on a Monday, just as today is. He was born in the afternoon in the hospital at Fort Ord, California, just across the bay from where I was attending the Army Language School at the Presidio of Monterey. I took Barbara to the hospital that morning before I went to class, took her to where she needed to be, and then I was told to go back to the office and "have orders cut so the baby could be born".

Friday afternoon I was to pickup Barbara and Ken, but Friday afternoons is when I had to stand parade retreat inspection at the Presidio. So, I went to see the company commander, a second lieutenant, and asked permission to skip the inspection so I could go to the hospital "to bring my wife and newborn infant home". "What is it, a boy or girl?" the lieutenant asked. "It's a son, sir", I replied. "Alright, since it's a boy, you have permission to skip the retreat and inspection. If it was a girl, she could wait until after inspection". (That was in 1950. Could the lieutenant get away with that today?) Anyway, I went to the hospital, paid the $7.00 bill and took Barbara and Kenneth home. We were living upstairs in a nice old house near the edge of Pacific Grove in Monterey. When we got home Paul and Lea, Barbara's parents, were waiting for us to drive up. And being a proud grandmother anxious to see her first grandchild, Lea was immediately there to open the door for Barbara and get Kenneth into her arms. As soon as they were satisfied everything was in order, and it didn't take long – never did – the Stoakins were in their car and on their way back to Los Angeles.

A little while after Barbara, Kenneth and I were upstairs in our apartment here was a knock on the door. It was a little Girl Scout, who asked, "Does Kenneth Severin live here?" "Yes, he lives here." "Okay, here is a box of Girl Scout cookies fro him from his friend Henry Franzoni". The little girl gave me the box of cookies and left.

Henry (Hank) Franzoni was a classmate at the Army Language School and a good friend, often coming over on Friday evenings to play bridge. The little Girl Scout had been by his place selling cookies, and he bought a box and then asked her to deliver it to Kenneth. So, whenever I see Girl Scout cookies being sold I know it's about time for Kenneth's birthday. Memories, Memories!!!

Here's another memory, this one 35 years ago today, Kenneth's 15th birthday. One March 7, 1970, there was a solar eclipse, a total eclipse. The center of the path of the eclipse went over Wilson, North Carolina, about 200 miles south of us.

One of Kenneth's earliest interests was astronomy, and as with anything he was interested in, it was serious. It was only natural that Ken would build a telescope for himself. He did, build two of them, a 4 inch and an 8 inch, did all the work himself, everything, including polishing the lenses, aligning them, etc. He went to astronomy classes to learn what he could. Nothing half way.

Anyway, to celebrate his 15th birthday, we loaded Kenneth, one of his school friends, David Keto, and his telescopes into our International Travelall, and drove to North Carolina to be able to see the eclipse at its fullest. A good time had by all.

This reminds me that one of the reasons we bought this place, where we are, is because of Ken's interest in astronomy. Ken wanted a place to mount his telescopes, so he dug a 4 foot hole and set a pipe in concrete, set it that way in order to minimize vibrations, so he could set up the telescopes in the right way. Ken has been gone from home since 1973, for all intents and purposes, and his telescope area, which he floored with bricks and railroad ties, now has cedars and poplar trees 20 feet tall in it. Can't see much sky from there now anyway.

Chapter 10

THOSE LASTING IMPRESSIONS

One must have lived greatly, whose record would bear the full light of day from beginning to its close.
   Amos Bronson Alcott, *Table Talk-Learning*

I HURTED SO BAD I NO COULD CRY
Thelma Webb Wright

Things in my childhood often happened that puzzled me with no understanding, acceptance or meaning. Then, as an adult, an event would emerge, and wham, there would be a flashback that would give understanding and meaning to a puzzle of my childhood. With the understanding I would often benefit emotionally.

I was a child standing on top of a mound of dirt watching the Italian ditch digger Dad had hired to dig a ditch for a pipe line. He was standing in the ditch, leaning on the shovel telling me a story in broken English. The words I remembered were, *"I hurted so bad I no could cry."* In my child mind I couldn't understand how one could not cry if hurt.

It was a hot evening in July 1944 when my neighbor decided it was time to drive me to Mountainside Hospital in Montclair, New Jersey. We giggled walking up the steps. I was going to have my first baby! And what did a young 21 year old girl in 1944 know about having a baby? Nothing! It was all a mystery. And it remained a mystery. I woke up in a room with three other new mothers and was told I had a healthy six pound baby girl born on July 25.

I waited, without questions, to see Jacqueline Yvonne Wright. I was too drugged to question the unexpected visit of Dad from his Virginia home. He had little to say, he was just there. It was not until the second day when my husband, John, walked in that I felt something was wrong. He was in Army training in Mississippi, preparing to go overseas. The American Red Cross gave him money for an emergency leave.

I was placed in a private room, then, informed the doctor used high forceps to deliver Jackie. She was injured and died on the fourth day with forceps marks on her forehead. Dad returned to Virginia. I was taken to my apartment in an ambulance so John and I could have a few days alone before he returned to Biloxi, Mississippi to continue his training.

The baby that was to be my joy while waiting for John to return from war was not to be.

I did not cry.

I had a flashback of me as a child standing on top of a mound of dirt watching the Italian ditch digger standing in the ditch, leaning on his shovel and telling me a story in broken English.

I heard him say, *"I hurted so bad I no could cry."*

STORIES FROM THE PAST
Harriet Burgess

These are stories told to me by my maternal grandmother, Harriotte Lee Turberville-McWhorter, when I was growing up. My grandmother was born July 4, 1881 at Fairfax Courthouse, Va. and lived at the family home called "Leeton" near Chantilly, Va. She was raised by an elderly spinster aunt also named Harriotte Lee, as my grandmother's mother Adeline died in childbirth at the age of 36. Her father was a lawyer at Fairfax Courthouse and a 'gentleman farmer', with hired help to work the farm.

Her early education was spent being tutored by a governess there at Leeton, learning the 3 Rs and comportment (the art of behaving like a lady). Later she was sent two miles down the road to Cabell's Mill, which was a one-room schoolhouse and attended by a few neighboring children. They were taught Latin, French and other advanced studies. Of course transportation was supplied by horse and buggy if the family horse Lord Fairfax was cooperative. Her childhood was a happy one, growing up with a sister and two brothers..

When she was 21 she had met and married my grandfather Pinckney Lee McWhorter. Her family didn't approved of their relationship and so they ran away to be married. The story goes they made their way over the Virginia border with the family in hot pursuit. At the border the police took pity on the young couple and let them continue on. They were married in Fort Mill, S.C. by Rev. W. A. Wright on January 1, 1903. Apparently Pinckney had worked in this area in earlier years.

Upon returning home to Leeton, Harriotte Lee's father gave her 100 acres of adjoining land where she and Pinckney built their home, across a field from Leeton. There they had three children, Margaret (my mother), George and Bill.

Hard times were knocking at the door there in Virginia around 1910 and Grandfather McWhorter headed west to look for work. His occupation was that of a stone mason but he worked at many other types of jobs. He found work near Yuma, Arizona and ended up helping to build Laguna Dam for the U.S. Reclamation Service. He sent for his family and Grandmother told a story of the hardships of that trip west. The youngest child, Bill, was sick and was always puny, so he was fretful the whole trip. They boarded the train in Alexandria with only coach seats available. There she was with three little children traveling on limited income and certainly limited facilities. Other kindly riders helped her out by amusing the two other children and they finally arrived in Yuma after a 4-day trip across the country.

Grandfather met the train and transported them all by carriage to a small and barren community called Potholes, near the dam location. It consisted of a few frame houses, barren desert, cactus taller than a human, and lots of mosquitoes. The population consisted of a few Anglo supervisors and their families, and mostly Mexican workers. The family settled in and Grandmother got to know the other wives and families. The hot weather in Yuma was often over 100 degrees and the family on weekends would catch a train and escape to LaJolla, California for the cool ocean breezes. Also while living in the Yuma area, Grandmother related the thrill of seeing Wild Bill Hickok's Wild West Show. Granddad would often go hunting in the desert with the Mexicans for wild bulls and even jackrabbits. Later they moved to Yuma where there was even grass in the yard, as the weather got unbearable in Potholes.

Grandmother McWhorter and children with sister Mary, Potholes, Arizona, 1911

Family at house in Yuma, Arizona, 1911

Pinckney McWhorter (left) with electric lines built at Acmar, Alabama, c 1914

Pinckney McWhorter at job site of Eufala Dam, Alabama, c. 1915

Upon completion of Laguna Dam in 1911 the family headed back to their home in Chantilly, Va. where life resumed. Grandfather still had to find work in far distant places and Grandmother and kids would join him from time to time near these jobs. One such job found him erecting electric and telephone lines at Acmar, Alabama. Another job took him to Muscle Shoals, Alabama where he worked on the Muscle Shoals Dam and mill foundation with a pump station. Another location was a dam at Eufala, Alabama where the family again joined him for a time.

Eventually the economy improved in the Fairfax area and Grandfather was able to pursue his vocation of stone mason, building stone fences, stone houses and various other structures in the nearby communities, i.e. Middleburg, Herndon, Manassas, Centerville and Fairfax. He never learned to drive so in later years he had to rely on others for transportation—often with fellow workers. Many times he would catch a ride as far as Centerville and walk the remaining three miles home. One of his jobs took him to Washington, D.C. where he worked on the National Cathedral.

At this time Grandmother was raising four children, Sam having joined the family after they came back from Yuma. (He was never suppose to happen as Grandmother was told she couldn't have any more children, but there he was anyway and much beloved).

Grandmother became a dairy farmer and raised Holstein cows, pigs, and crops of wheat, corn, hay and lots of chickens. When the farm got too much for her in later years she raised beef cattle as there was less work involved. Grandfather never cared for the life of a farmer and he continued with his stone mason work. It all worked out well.

In their declining years the youngest son Sam took over the farm work until World War II when he joined the Merchant Marines. The other brothers joined the Army, Bill fighting in Europe with Gen. Patton and George in the Pacific. All came home thankfully. Life continued on at the farm with hired help as all the sons had married and left home and the beef cattle remained the main livelihood. Grandfather died in 1949 at the age of 74. Grandmother lived on until 1962 and died at age 81. They are both buried in the family cemetery at Leeton.

ETCHED IN MEMORY
Eugene Tucker

Our journey through life is filled with numerous events and experiences. Many of which have left lasting impressions that we are likely to carry throughout our lives. As a young child I would sit at the feet of my parents and grandparents at every opportunity to listen to their stories, many of which were handed down from their parents and grandparents. Our little house was without running water or electricity, so our entertainment was the stories being told by our elders. We were not permitted to speak, for this would be a sign of disrespect and would lead to a quick dismissal or even a spanking. So, we would sit in silence with our imagination racing as we peered into the dark room trying to see the expressions on the faces of our elders and their animated motions-- hands and arms flailing about, voices changing to imitate a person or animal, standing with contortions to demonstrate the action of someone or something. Each one would have a different story to tell as they tried to upstage the other. Sometimes the discussions would become quite heated over the details of some of the stories. After all many of these stories came from shared memories and their recollections were probably a little different. Who was right or wrong mattered little for us small children. How they resolved the differences and moved to other stories were the real lessons we learned from these encounters with our elders. As I look back some sixty years later this was theatre in its purest form and what great actors these people were, but their stories and their messages were real, for they had lived them, and had passed them on to us. However, we would never be able to share the stories with the same intensity of emotion as our elders. We had received them vicariously. They had lived them. Today, as we try to retell these stories, they are received as myths for this generation of children have no reference point and these stories are too far removed for their reality.

As I sat at the feet of my elders I could feel the sadness of their plight during my grandmother and their mothers and fathers time in slavery. They told stories of being fed from troughs like pigs, working from sun up to sundown, mothers dragging cotton sacks in the fields while carrying their new born children on their backs, the beheading of my great great uncles and the placing of their heads on gate posts as reminders for stealing food, the moaning of slaves being beaten for not following rules or reaching their day's quotas, the screams of mothers whose children were taken away and sold. Then there were stories about lynching. My mother's school mates, the Pastor taken from his Church, my mother hiding under her bed while a Negro man was being torched and lynched in the nearby woods. Many had gathered to witness the event that went on for hours while the man's helpless body draped from a tree with his private parts cut out, finger torched off, and a fire build under him for the final episode of the poor creatures' life. For years I would wonder if life was so precious that slavery was a better alternative than death. *What would this legacy mean for me and my off springs?* For a question that was raised in the nineteenth century there is no clear answer in the twenty first century.

As years passed I too began to understand that I was also the focal point of a great social debate. Many of the issues that confronted my elders were being played out in a different format. Now there were laws that were being formed and challenged that dealt with my elders and me. The issue as to whether or not I was a "man" was being debated. *Was I only three-fifths of a man?* The word freedom began to have meaning for me. I had not thought much about being sent to the back of the bus or having to go to "colored schools". I found no fault with having to go to "my Church" or to live in "my community". For me this was a state of nature. I was not aware of my limitations, since my parents, relatives and neighbors had not told me. Now, I was confronted with daily news accounts of the national social debate, the consequences often fatal for many of my kind, and the divide this was causing our country. Perhaps, President Lincoln had not really freed the slave, but rather placed him in a different stage of bondage. I listened to the passionate speeches of Dr. Martin Luther King, Jr., the congressional debates over civil rights laws, witnessed the marches in the streets across the south, the denial of children trying to "integrate" schools. I began to understand the "fight for freedom" and how little freedom I had. Yet, the freedom I had was far more than other peoples of the world that I had read about in my history books. Now, I had a dilemma. *Do I rise up in protest as so many others were doing, or do I remain silent and wage my own private war against prejudice?* Marching was too dangerous; nonviolence did not fit my personality. So, I decided to remain invisible and silently applaud those with the boldness to march with Dr. King while my soul burned with each image of the hoses, cattle prods, night sticks, and dogs attacking those brave warriors asking for freedom and justice on the very soil my ancestors had shed their blood, sweat and tears. Confrontation and bloodshed were not answers for me. For the oppressor's violence, intimidation, and empty promises had worked well in the past. But now the socially oppressed genie had grown too large to be stuffed back into its bottle. It had reached the world stage with all eyes and ears focused on its eventual outcome. A simple and honest answer to the question "Why do you hate me?" could trigger a dialogue for freedom for all Americans and could have sent a most compelling message to all the world. However, the question could not be asked for no one was willing to listen. It was like, go ahead and speak, but I am not listening, so that I can continue with what I was saying. The eloquence of oratory had not been heard on this land since those laudatory utterances in the House of the Burgesses from those seeking freedom from England. One patriot stood and uttered these words

> *"What is it that Gentlemen wish? What would they have? Is life so dear or peace so sweet as to be purchased at the price of chains and slavery? Forgive them All Mighty God for I know not what course others may take, but as for me give me liberty or give me death".* (Patrick Henry)

Perhaps, this was the mantra with which the Dr. King marchers took to the streets. So the marchers continued to march, the oppressors continued in hot pursuit, while people like me continued to work in silence. One day the oppressor would ask in surprise

> *"How did you get here, you were not invited to sit at my table?"*

On November 23, 1963, I was sitting in my ground floor office at the Internal Revenue Service facing the Justice Department along 12th Street in Washington, DC. Usually I could look out of my window and see Robert Kennedy, the US Attorney General and brother of the President, when he arrived in his second floor office with his big dog. The day began like any other day for me. I was consumed with the problem of how to develop an algorithm to detect erroneous social security numbers. I don't recall seeing Robert Kennedy on this day. By mid day a dark cloud seemed to engulf my very being and everything around me. The President of The United States had been shot and killed in Dallas, Texas. As I walked north along 12th street towards Pennsylvania Avenue I began to internalize the meaning of the term "sounds of silence". My inner reflections masked everything and everyone on the streets that day. Gone was the man who had heard the call of my elders and had dared to seek a place for me at the table. Now what? I had braved the cold on his Inauguration Day in January 1960 standing only a few yards from the podium, and heard his challenge to the peoples of our country *"Ask not what your County can do for you, but what you can do for your Country."* On this day this was my Country too. Now it was time to stand along the parade route on Pennsylvania Avenue and witness the horse drawn caisson bearing his flag draped bier, followed by a rider less horse darned with boots pointed back towards the White House from whence it came signifying a fallen soldier and the cortège of dignitaries marching towards the Capitol Building of The United States. There was his widow, Jackie, draped majestically in black with a veil covering her sadden face, holding the hands of her children, Caroline and John John. Their short journey as Head of State would now end at Arlington Cemetery in nearby Virginia, so would the image of Camelot. *Would my journey towards freedom end here too?*

This event would be the beginning of a series of events that would frame the answer to my question. Dr. Martin Luther King, Jr. would be killed in Memphis,

Tennessee; Robert Kennedy would be killed in California. Medgar Evers would be killed in Mississippi, Malcolm X in Chicago, and many other heinous crimes would be perpetrated against those who dared to march along the highways and roads throughout the South all well documented and reported for the world to see.

This was the 1960's and I declared that I was more than three-fifths of a man.

LAW, FOR WHOM?
Eugene Tucker

Nigger, if you keep your black ass out of the grave, I'll keep you out of jail! This was the pledge given to Negroes by employers in Grenada, Mississippi during the 1930's and 40's. However, this pledge only applied to Negroes having conflicts with other Negroes. Immediate death by lynching would be the consequence, if a Negro sassed or killed a White person. This was how I remembered my elders' warnings during my early years. There were two sets of laws. One set for us and one for everyone else. The more learned among us understood that there was a criminal justice system that presumed innocence until proven guilty in a court of law before a judge or a jury of your peers. Throughout my youth and into adulthood I witnessed breaches in these fundamental rights governing our society. Evidence and proof seemed unimportant for Black suspects. Your color made you a suspect whether or not you were nowhere in the vicinity of a crime. You fit the description, charged with the crime and found guilty and punished. It was assumed that all Black men looked the same. Murder against another Black person would in most cases result in a few days to a few months in jail. Parole was generously granted.

My Uncle Charlie was ambushed and shot dead in Louisville, Kentucky in the 1970's by his irate son-in-law for "interfering in his marriage" and then critically injuring his wife during the same rampage. Less than two months later he walked the streets a free man. Any alleged crime against a White woman almost always resulted in the death penalty. In the late 1950's a cousin noticed a young Black man and white girl rendezvous each evening near his orchard for several months. One evening a policeman in his squad car noticed the couple parked there and immediately arrested the young man. The girl was forced to say that the young man raped her. The young Black man was found guilty and put to death in the electric chair. My cousin was afraid to come forward and testify for fear of retribution. You may get lucky and receive a long prison term or death if you committed a crime against a White male. There was no such thing as Miranda Rights then. We could not afford lawyers anyway and if the courts appointed one to us, there would be no effort made to protect our legal rights. If you were Black, you did not want to become at issue with the law.

In Mississippi a criminal case involving crimes against a Black person by Whites usually resulted in a circus atmosphere in the court room. Peers of White suspects were members from the community and shared the same disposition towards Black people as those involved in the crimes. No White person would ever be found guilty for violating or lynching a Black person and in most cases suspects would never be found. It has taken over forty years and public outcry to finally bring closure on a horrific crime committed against a teenage boy in Lucky, Mississippi for allegedly whistling at a White woman.

Through the years many laws were passed giving rights to equal housing, transportation, employment, and entrance to public places. These laws were not always observed. I was thrilled to be permitted to obtain a library card and enter the public library in 1953. I was denied housing in the Nation's capital and in Northern Virginia in the 1960's. In the 1980's I witnessed the plight of Black citizens in Alexandria, Virginia trying to hold on to their property against the planning commission and developers confiscating their land. The city with its authority continued to raise property taxes and impose restrictions that made it difficult to maintain ownership of their property along the Potomac River and the surrounding area, now deemed prime for upscale development. The developed waterfront in Alexandria, Virginia is testimony to this crusade. I, too, would be a victim of this crusade.

REMEMBERING DAD
Helen P. Hannett

After my father was promoted to post surgeon and commanding officer of the dispensary on our army post in Texas, he shared with us his cultural interests. Preceding our move onto the post, he had been doing therapeutic things with his hands to help him recover from the physical effects of Bataan Death March followed by three and one-half year of torture and starvation as a Japanese prisoner of war both in the Philippines and Japan in World War II. The first things he gave my little brother and me after we were settled into our new house on post were handmade stuffed toys, Pluto and Donald Duck that he had made himself. They were intricate with a large number of pieces and made without a sewing machine. They were also a labor of love.

Daddy shared his love for music with us. One Sunday as we came in from church, Mother, with her dark curly hair pulled back and wearing a brown and whit polka dot dress, came over to me and my little brother smiling and radiating all the beauty of youth and love for my father. With the intelligence and presence of the best orchestra master of ceremonies, Mom said, *"Daddy has some violin music he had prepared for you and Michael. Be sure to thank Daddy after his concert as he has spent a lot of time preparing"*. Mike and I sat on our small red and blue painted Mexican chairs on the "Tree of Life" oriental rug in the living room and listened. Daddy stood in front of the living room fireplace with his music stand and his violin. Mother sat in a chair to our left. Daddy played a medley of nursery rhymes, including "Baa, Baa Black Sheep,"

Mike and me with Mom and Dad

"Twinkle, Twinkle, Little Star," and "Mary Had a Little Lamb". I actually was beyond nursery rhymes, as in our first year preschool class, we had learned all the verses of "The Eyes of Texas Are Upon You".

I knew that Daddy had studied the violin in high school. It was one of his hobbies along with the coronet back then. That day in our living room in our new house was the first and last time I ever heard him play a musical instrument. Mom set the tone of loving care. She had had a lot of experience as her older sister was a gifted and temperamental pianist. As a child, Mom had to accompany her to church when she practiced in order to help her by turning the pages of the organ music. Mother expected us to be an appreciative audience, and we were.

Mom, my brother and me

Although I wasn't three years old then, I can still remember the violin string sounds and how they sounded as Daddy played them. Dad played one nursery rhyme after another with flourish and spirit. I have to admit that although I thanked Daddy afterwards, I didn't really like the sound of the violin. I wish I had understood the effort it took. I can not have known then how much time he spent practicing that music just for us and how much love had gone into it. I've always felt badly that I never thanked him enough because of all that love.

I was a bit startled by the sound of the violin and preferred the sound of the piano. If I could go back and just let him know how really wonderful he was. Dad didn't play again for us after that, but he kept sharing beautiful music with me. His concert helped to spark within me a love for beautiful music. In the early grades he bought me one album a month like *Sparkey's Magic Piano* with *"The flight of the Bumblebee"* and Schehezerade. He would delight that I loved Liberacci and the songs of Perry Como, such as "Don't Let the Stars Get In Your Eyes". When I studied ballet later and immersed my childhood in it, I always had a Tchaikowsky record on, either *Swan Lake, The Nutcracker Suite,* or *Sleeping Beauty* that Daddy had bought.

A teenage babysitter had taught me and my brother the waltz, so then I started listening to all Dad's Strauss waltzes. From waltzes it was easy to move into polkas. Dad played polkas often on his record player. The beauty of the waltzes and polkas as opposed to the ballet music was that Daddy and I could dance the waltzes and polkas together. In fact, my brother, sister, mother, father, and I all danced them. The polka we considered part of our Polish and Ukrainian heritage.

My father communicated through music. When I was in high school, some uncool rock and roll records arrived in the mail, my brother and I laughed mercilessly at the weird music and wondered who could have possibly sent it. I felt badly because I thought I knew who sent it, and he could hear us laughing about it. We didn't receive any more records in the mail, but one day Dad got us tickets to the Beetles when they came to Washington, DC. The flashes from all of the spectators' cameras could have illuminated the Beetles without spotlights, and we all had a wonderful evening with beautiful memories of that concert.

Did I mention that my family sang everywhere we went? Well, we did like so many families did then. Whenever we drove anywhere in the car, we would all harmonize. Mother and I could sing different parts than soprano. The family traveling songfests gave us considerable joy.

I was a teenager in college when Daddy gave me the last records—heartbreaking wartime love songs of a soldier to his child: "The Ballard of the Green Beret: and the song on the flip side, "Go to Bed, It's Getting Late". As army children in post World War II America, we thought nothing could ever hurt us or our fathers. Daddy gave me the record before he left for a brief trip to war torn Vietnam where he would inspect the army hospitals and supervise our doctors there. Dad was expert in tropical diseases from treating American soldiers during WWII in the Philippines and Japan.

I listened to both sides of that record hundreds of times, most likely driving everyone around me crazy in the college dorm. I wept for the soldiers in the songs who cried as they kissed their sleeping children goodbye before leaving in the middle of the night for Vietnam. It never occurred to me that those songs would be Daddy's farewell love song to me if he lost his life over there, too. I was so carefree that I never remembered worrying. My girlfriend Cathy's father was ordered to Vietnam for about a year, and she didn't worry either. However, I do remember the solemnity with which Daddy hugged me goodbye; he returned safely though a few weeks later.

There were many beautiful songs in the sixties. Even though my husband David and I met at the Officers' Club Swimming Pool when we were twenty—he was a lifeguard—we fell in love through music. David would loan me his albums of Broadway musicals. Those musicals communicated warmth, grace, and love.

In 1982 when my father lay in the hospital dying from Alzheimer's disease, Mom told me that she had a gift from Dad for me. It was a piano they had bought from a friend and put in storage when they retired. Then Mom took it out of storage and had it transported to my living room. I was so overjoyed with this gift.

When I was eight years old, I had taken a semester of piano. Since we didn't have a piano then, I was greatly frustrated. Now, suddenly at 35 years old I had one. What happened then was an artistic surge. After twelve hours of lessons from a friend over three month time span and hours of daily practice, I learned how to play the piano. My first piece was Schubert's "Ave Maria". In loving my father and mourning for him, I found the power and motivation to learn to play all the beautiful songs that we sang or listened to together in the past, that he and mother loved and listened to, and songs popular during the 1950's. My method of learning during that three month time period was simply to pick a song I really wanted to play, and the teacher would show me everything I needed to know to play it. That's how I progressed. After those three months in 1982, I had learned enough from this song by song method to carry me for the next twenty or more years adding to my repertoire by self teaching.

Spring Is On The Way
Keith Severin

Hello! Hello! February 27, 2005

It's just after one o'clock in the next-to-last afternoon of February. I just came in from bringing the horses from the back pasture, and based on what I saw I guess you could say that spring is on the way. According to the calendar, it arrives in three weeks.

Yes, I saw a robin, the first one this year, out working in the neighbor's cattle pasture. The bird was alone, but I'm sure there are others. Having seen that robin, I took a closer look at the horses, at their coats especially. There are still lots of horse hair out there, none shedded yet. But, on the other hand, I did see a patch of crocus in bloom this morning, their gentle yellow-gold and blue flowers showing through a skim of snow. Actually, it was more than a week ago, on the 16th, that I saw the first crocus in bloom. It looked pretty lonely. The several days after that, I noticed that it had closed up, a tight bud there in the weather that had gotten colder. Spring is on the way.

In three weeks we can be on the lookout for the woodducks that normally appear on March 20-21, 3-4 pairs of them here on the upper pond just below the house. And a month after that, about April 21st we can expect to see the hummingbirds. Have to get the feeders out and ready for them.

The last several mornings this week I have seen 2 pairs of ducks on the lower pond – can't tell if they are woodies or mallards. Can't see too well there since I'm walking into the sun and they are in the shadow on the pond bank. They are there, though. Also, on some mornings there are about 4 pairs of Canadian geese in the pasture above the pond.

Another observation from the other day was that I noticed there were no birds around. Strange, since it was cold and I thought they would have been around the feeders. Then, I noticed a little hawk sitting quietly in a tree not far from the carport. I was there to put the trash into the can. The hawk just sat and watched me, not offering to be scared off. Then, it took off to another nearby tree. It just sat quietly waiting for…

Today is the first day I've felt close to being totally human in more than 2 weeks. I came home from Chicago two weeks ago today with the beginnings of what was a serious cold. For the next 10-12 days I spent part or all day in bed. Curious, I had no fever, no aches, or pains, or sore throat, or chest, just coughing, coughing fits that would hit very suddenly. Cough drops or cough syrup of no help.   Water was the only thing that seemed to help. I had no appetite, either. Finally, last Tuesday I called the doctor – my man, Dr. McCue at Mountainside Medicine up near Little Washington in the edge of the Blue Ridge Mountains, about 45 minutes from us. He looked at me and said, "You've got it."   I asked what "it" was. First, a cold, then the flu, and now getting close to pneumonia.   He gave me some strong antibiotic pills and some syrup. The effect was immediate, gradual but steady. So…

   Today, I cleared the ice off the front steps, cut some firewood, split some too, put new county inspection stickers on the cars' windshields, and did some other things. Nearly human, but I do want to sleep, stay in bed. Nearly human – how good it feels!

Chapter 11

LIFE SHAPING EVENTS

Where we live or how we live is of little consequence.
What is important is to live.
          Ernest Dimnet, *What we live by*

Eisenhower, Daddy, and Me
Helen P. Hannett

It was autumn of 1960. Dad was 49, and I was 13. We had returned to the mainland from Oahu, Hawaii in the preceding summer of 1959 after my grandfather had died. Dad was stationed in nearby Virginia. There was a feeling that President Eisenhower was a lame duck, and there was a fascination and preoccupation with Mr. Kennedy's beauty and sophistication.

One day midway between the 1960 Presidential Campaign and the inauguration of John F. Kennedy in 1961, Dad asked if I'd like to drive out to Walter Reed Army Hospital to visit a patient there. We drove over in our two tone green 98 Olds that had taken us across the country once in 1956 and back again in 1959. I spent the whole drive reading and thinking about "Jackie," the President's wife. Dad listened to the radio, and I was hoping that the song, "High Hopes," would come on. The drive over was uneventful as we made the pleasant drive through Washington, D.C. to the old red brick military hospital on Georgia Avenue. I had accompanied Dad a number of times, and it was always nice just to be with him when he made his social visits to patients. After which he would study their charts.

This day Dad only made one call. It was to a patient who suffered from premature aging and would need to have his veins stripped. It really surprised me that the illness left the patient looking several decades older than he actually was. Dad then walked down the hall to a room which contained empty glass vials and patient record folders. It was still and quiet and I followed him in and waited while he pulled out a couple of charts and read.

Dad was still reading when I heard the quiet footsteps of a young officer who entered the small room. Dad looked up, and the officer spoke to my father and asked, "Colonel would your daughter like to meet President Eisenhower?" Even today, 43 years later, I still get goose bumps thinking of those words.

We only had a few seconds, and Daddy and I accompanied the officer, turning right then down the hall and then left into the Presidential Suite. In the doorway of the Presidential Suite, I noticed how big it was—about the size of four bedrooms set side by side. There were three or four people, doctors and secret service men inside. In the far right hand corner there was a hospital bed with the back raised. Sitting there in a hospital gown covered by a blanket and a bedspread was President Dwight Eisenhower. Dad and I stopped at the foot of the bed. I was at the foot on Eisenhower's right side, and Dad, at the foot, on Eisenhower's left.

I wasn't nervous then, but I get butterflies now just thinking about it. From the time the president saw me in the doorway, he looked directly into my eyes in a kind and friendly way. He was presented to me and looked into my eyes talking to me as I stood with Dad at the foot of his bed. "I have grandchildren your age," Eisenhower said. It was comfortable to be there with him, even though I was timid.

The child raising philosophy of the day was "Children are seen and not heard." What I was thinking of telling him but I knew it would be too stupid to say was that I saw in a newspaper photograph how two of his granddaughters and I wore the same outfit at Easter time. It was a pink and gray wool plaid suit with big wide pleats. That was on my mind, but it would have been too boring to say to him.

Eisenhower looked so kind with a young face and friendly eyes. He was about one or two years younger than my grandfather, who had seemed old to me because he was my grandfather. Both were born between 1887 and 1890.

If it had been Mr. Truman there, I would have been thinking, "thanks for bringing my father home from the war by deciding to drop the bomb before I was born". I have a deep love for Truman because he ended my father's suffering as a more than three year POW of the Japanese and brought back all the men. The Japanese would not stop even surrender after the first bombing.

Eisenhower was the candidate we all supported in the past elections. I told Dad I was for Eisenhower when he ran in his last election because "he wouldn't give the country away to communism." Dad wholeheartedly agreed with me.

I could have told the president that we lived in Hawaii when he signed the papers declaring Hawaii the 50th state of the union. We felt the joy of the people colorfully dressed in muumuus, aloha shirts, and leis as all the bells rang out all over the island. We had sat under stars on July 4th, 1959, on the grounds around the Washington Monument and for the first time ever saw a stand-up pyrotechnic display of a U.S. flag sparkling brightly with 50 burning stars. All I did was look into his kind eyes and answer his questions. It was comfortable being around him. That was the wonder, and that was enough.

Eisenhower and my father spoke for a while in words that were too soft and foreign for me to understand and probably were in military and medical terms. I could feel my father's love, awe, and reverence for the man, commander-in-chief and who as Commanding General of Allied Forces in Europe during World War II helped America win the war. I could also feel Eisenhower's love and respect for my father. This gift Eisenhower possessed was why troops and our nation loved him and followed him.

Eisenhower at this stage of his life was looking to account for the good he had done in his life: the soldiers he helped bring home, the lives saved by defeating Hitler, and all of the children subsequently born in peacetime. In addition, having recently lost his own beloved father, I feel my Dad experienced an uplift in being in the presence of a man who was a contemporary of his own father who radiated a genuine paternal concern and who was also a great leader and American president.

Events That Shape My Life
Eugene Tucker

Learning To Read
"Reading maketh a full man; writing a ready man; and conference an exact man. And if a man reads little, he had need know that he doeth not." Unknown

I do not know when I learned to read with comprehension, since I was not a participant in my early years in school. At a very early age my sister, Leona, and I would play school. Looking at pictures in the old magazines and papers we had around the house was the source of inspiration and imagination. We began matching words with pictures and asking questions and listening to conversations between our elders and our older sisters. I think by sheer will we forced ourselves to read words and to put our own interpretation on their meaning. Our parents recognized our determination and provided us with books on many subjects written on many levels, most of which were well beyond our age level. This was their way satisfying our appetite for learning things that they were not able to explain. That mattered little to us as our house filled with books. Our parents also invested in a set of Britannica Encyclopedias which they purchased from a door to door salesman, dictionaries, and books on human biology, history, Vogue Magazines, history of art, and so many others. What treasures we had around us and what extraordinary parents. There could never be enough praise and credit given to these two people.

The Weekly Reader
Every week during my elementary school days I looked forward to seeing *The Weekly Reader,* a small news bulletin for children. Our teacher would review with the class all of the news of the month and we would have a discussion about many of the stories, after we pledged allegiance to the flag and sang the Negro National Anthem. It was here I learned about Ralph Bunch and the United Nations and the construction of the Pennsylvania Turnpike. The Turnpike would be built and financed by tolls which were to last for a certain period of time. Someone forgot about the period of time, for the tolls lingers today and have increased, perhaps, due to inflation. I learned about Marion Anderson, the contralto singer; Paul Robeson, actor and singer; DuBoise, author, the first Negro to earn a PhD from Harvard and founder of the NAACP; and many other important Negro Americans. This was our Black History long before a date was set aside to honor Dr. Martin Luther King, Jr. Our teachers demonstrated to us that our color should not be a barrier and challenged us to pursue knowledge. Knowledge was our freedom.

First Library Card

What a thrill it was to walk into the main library on fourth and Guthrie Street in Louisville, Kentucky and receive a library card. No Negro in this city had been permitted such a privilege. We had always been issued text books that had been discarded by White children. Some were in good shape; others were marked and torn and generally unusable. Our teachers were the front line soldiers against prejudice. Even though I was nearing the end of my high school career, obtaining a library card opened a new and exciting chapter in my life. Our teachers coached us on what it meant to have a library card, the Dewey Decimal System, the card catalogue, library ethics, and the wonderful world of knowledge bound between the pages of all these books. I had read Benjamin Franklin's *Poor Richards Almanac* and recalled some of its passages, one saying in particular:

"If a man empties his purse into his head, no man can take it away from him. An investment in knowledge always pays the best interest."

My first day in the library was quite tense as people stared at me. I guess they were wondering if I would steal a book, tear out pages, or speak above a whisper. I remember rummaging through the shelves and found a book titled "A Spanish Tragedy" written by Thomas Kyd some years before Shakespeare's *Othello*. This book had not been taken from the shelves since 1940. As I thumbed through the book I quickly say that the story had the same plot and some of the same characters as the Shakespeare's play. This would be the first book I checked out of the library. I was always fascinated by Shakespeare and the controversy surrounding the authorship of some of his work. I also found an account of the flood titled Ut Napistim which parallels the biblical story of Noah and the Ark, a story written thousands of miles from the site of the biblical account. Today we search the universe to satisfy man's hunger for knowledge and to rewrite many of the books now occupying the shelves of our libraries.

Grandma's Race Card

Leona and I graduated from high school at the same time as our cousin, Robbie. Robbie was the daughter of our aunt Mary Anna, who continued to live in Grenada, Mississippi, where Grandma lived. Robbie was a beautiful light skin, with many admirable social graces. She played several musical instruments including piano and saxophone and was pleasant to be around. We always admired her and looked forward to seeing her when we returned to Mississippi. Her fair skin made her a favorite of Grandma, who had lived through a period in our nation's history which had taught her to believe that skin color made a difference between success and failure. Grandma's desire to see her offsprings and their children succeed was compelling. So, she decided the Robbie was the better choice to give her support to. Grandma had heard about Leona and me and told Momma

"You have some smart chaps!"

Robbie would enroll at Dillard University and major in music. I am so proud of Robbie's accomplishments as an educator. She has spent all of her adult life in Yazoo City, Mississippi and still calls me Baby Brother. My sister, Leona, would go on to receive a Medal of Honor from President Jimmy Carter as being one of the most outstanding women in the United States for her work in foreign trade. We understood that Grandma, too, had been victimized by racism and the consequences of slavery in ways I am beginning to fully understand. This would be a burden I also carry as I struggle to emerge from darkness.

Family Matters

Leona and I were "baby brother and baby sister" to all our family, relatives, neighbors and friends. We were thought of as twins even in school and by universities that would eventually seek us out. Of all the legions of cousins, aunts, and uncles, Leona and I were spoken of the most often. Our work habits, inquisitiveness, manners, and generosity quickly became known. As a child I was shy and impulsive; Leona was reserved and cautious. One day I alarmed my mother when I decided to crawl without any prior indications, then as abruptly I started to walk and talk. Leona refused to walk until she was three. Mom and Dad tried to determine why Leona would not walk. So, one day after a rainfall Dad took her out in her pretty dress near a puddle of water and stood a few feet away from her and called to her to come. Leona stood there for a while and decided to walk rather than sit in the puddle of water. As we grew older people throughout our neighborhood took notice of these two children. Whenever our elders visited our house we would sit in the corner to listen to their conversations, while their children played in the yard. By the time we were ten and eleven many adults would seek our advice on all types of topics ranging from the bible to "how to fix it". One neighbor tried to encourage me to challenge a radio evangelist who was challenging anyone who could dispute his claims among which one was that he would die and be reborn in the flesh according to scriptures. For some reason my neighbor thought I was capable to take such a challenge. The evangelist died and we are still waiting for the resurrection.

My cousin, Mr. Whitfield, used me as an example for his four boys.

"See Baby Brother, I want you to watch what he does and be like him!"

I was not aware of this challenge to his sons until many years later when one of the sons started to bring his new born children to see me. He now brings the grandchildren and their parents every year to visit me. I did not realize the extent of the burden that had been placed on me from childhood by my family or the number of people whose lives were affected by us. I knew of their love, support and devotion. I did not realize they saw me and Leona as their hope to survive slavery and pave the way for generations to come. I often ask myself ***"What if I had failed?"***

A TEST OF FAITH
Eugene Tucker

Massey Zion Baptist Church was a small church with about thirty pews, a vestibule at the entrance that could accommodate some ten people, a pulpit at the front of the sanctuary flanked by two choir stands, one for the senior choir and the other for the junior choir. There was a dressing room located behind the pulpit that were closed off by two entrance doors, where the choir robed and the pastor prepared for service. There was a rear side door where the choir could enter without entering the front of the church. The church was approximately forty feet wide and sixty feet long. There was a baptismal pool underneath the senior choir stand located to the right of the pulpit. The church was heated by a large black pot belly wood and coal burning stove located on the left side of the church in front of the senior choir stand. It was a chore keeping the church warm during the winter. An electric fan and paper fans with the logos of funeral parlors were used by the congregation during the hot summer days. Someone would have to mind the stove from time to time to make sure that the fire did not go out. The outside walls of the building were covered with red artificial brick siding. The church resembled an "A" frame house from a distance with a cross firmly anchored from the roof. The church sat on a parcel of land at the entrance to Tie Plant, a company town just outside of the city limits of Louisville, Kentucky on Bells Lane. Tie Plant was distinguished by its smell of hot creosote that emanated from processing of cross ties used for train tracks and light poles. A small stream ran through the little compound of shanties and wound its way under a portion of our Massey Zion Baptist Church. The church was built on cement blocks and bricks like most of the structures in the compound. The tiny stream would fill with water on occasion and would bring the overflow of creosote from the plant with it. The odor of creosote lingered forever darkening the soil and preserving every structure it touched including the church and all the houses in the compound. Members of the church who were residents of the compound had built the church and from all appearances had difficulty maintaining it.

My family had moved to Louisville, Kentucky to live in Tie Plant from Grenada, Mississippi in the 1940's. Tie Plant was an extension of the plant in Tie Plant, Mississippi. Many of the men who left Mississippi in search of a better opportunity found employment here. My father was one of them. My mother would dress Leona, my youngest sister, and me each Sunday and would take or send us off to this little church for

Sunday school and services. Services would last well into the afternoon and would often resume for evening services. I do not recall ever seeing my father inside this church. I later learned he had long sense given up on the power of faith. For him faith had not served him well over his years on this plain. There would be no tears, no prayers, no outward signs of anger, no show of passion, but one could see and feel signs of resignation on his face and in his body language. I could read him well. He was my Dad!

This little church became my Carnegie Hall, my minister the orchestra leader; my choir the opera. This was the place where theatrical performances were acted out; drama unfolded; comedy portrayed, a place where a value system was reinforced, and a sense of self was embedded for God loves us and we were somebody even under oppression, where hope of a better life if not on earth but in Heaven was ours for the choosing. It taught us to endure pain and suffering for in the end we win. Reverend W. G. Stamps was our minister and pastor. Rev. Stamps had come to this tiny outpost from a large church in the city of Louisville where he was an assistant minister. He had completed his studies at Simmons Bible College in Louisville and had taken this assignment in part, I think, to demonstrate his ability to lead a fledging flock and to make a difference. His mastery of psychology would serve him well in this place of creosote and tar. Reverend Stamps was a noble soul with a quiet demeanor, very fair of skin, a clean shaven round head, and always wore a three piece black suit, white shirt and dark necktie, and in winter was draped in a full length black overcoat. Tucked away in the pocket of his black vest was a Pullman's pocket watch attached to a long gold chain. He always carried himself like a preacher and his devotion to his faith was without question. This image of him would be with me throughout my life. Under his stewardship the little church would prosper and survive even attracting those outside the compound and keeping those who were fortunate to escape the compound and found better lives in the city. The church was even able to purchase a school bus to provide door-to-door service for those members scattered around the city. This bus was also used to transport children and their families during summer vacation from school to nearby scenic locations such as Mammoth Cave, Horse Cave, the Cincinnati Zoo and others. This was a special treat following Vacation Bible School, since we had no regular summer school programs and very little else to do.

It was here in this little church that one Sunday Reverend Stamps *"opened the doors of the Church"* for anyone willing to *"confess their sins and seek Jesus"* was asked to come forward to the front of the Church. Leona and I stepped forward with the strong approval of the congregation and were received into the Church. Our mother had transferred her membership to Massey Zion Baptist Church from her church in Grenada, Mississippi. We continued our religious training and prepared for our baptism. Baptismal services usually took place following the morning service sometime after one o'clock in the afternoon. This would be a life changing event for two children ages nine and ten. The floor of the senior choir stand had been lifted and the pool filled with water on the Saturday before Sunday services. Leona and I were anxious with trepidation about the impending event. We were not sure why we had taken this step. We knew the water was cold and deep and that our pastor was going to fully immerse us. What if he let go of us in that water? Now it was time for the event. Leona was dressed in a long white gown, I in pants and a white shirt. Reverend Stamps was dressed in a full body black rubber outfit which included rubber footies. He cautiously stepped into the pool with the assistance of one of the Deacons. The water was about waist high on Reverend Stamps, who said a prayer as the congregation who witnessed the event sang *"Take me to the water to be Baptized; None but the Righteous shall see God"* in a soft chant. When it was Leona's turn to get into the pool, I could see fear as she trembled when her feet touched the water. Reverend Stamps folded her hands over her chest and proceeded to calm her down. Then he said *"In the name of the Father, Son, and the Holy Ghost, I baptize you my sister!"* and he bent her backwards immersing her into the water. Leona came up fighting and gasping for breath, while the congregation voiced its approval saying *"Amen, Thank you Jesus!"* Someone said Leona's struggle was a sign that she was fighting off the devil. I think it was fear. I took my turn with *"manly courage"*, but I may have *"peed"* in my clothes. This would be a day never to be forgotten. As the years passed I began to understand the meaning of *"cosmic dualism"* and the need to continuously renew your faith. Reverend Stamps succeeded to teach me the meaning of good and evil from a religious perspective and what it meant to be spiritually free. The meaning of good and evil, honesty and freedom from a legal perspective would soon be learned as I witnessed the unfolding of justice in our legal system. If God was the higher authority, why did He not touch the hearts of those entrusted in making and implementing just laws for all His children? This dilemma only strengthened by faith, for no other reason that I feared the alternative. The Sunday school teachings, the voices of my elders, and the many examples of triumphs by ordinary people under seemingly impossible circumstances confirmed for me that good wins the battle over evil. One's faith shapes the man.

    This little church would become my sanctuary, my inspiration, my opportunity to explore my potential. I continued attending church here even after my family moved from Tie Plant and until I moved away from Louisville. The congregation of about one hundred consisted mostly of older women, and a few older men. The younger people were mostly female. Young men were at a premium. Reverend Stamps took notice of my devotion to the church and learned of my interest in learning. He also noticed my shyness and decided to trust me to teach a Sunday school class to the young adults. My success with this assignment lead to my being elected to be Superintendent of the Sunday School, a position traditionally held by someone more senior than I and with more training. However, not many could claim that they had read through the Bible and tried to understand its meaning. I could make this claim before I was seventeen years old. I could relive the stories and parables in my mind and questioned the wisdom and resolve the issues confronting the ancient writers to my own satisfaction. I believed that since God was the God of the Universe and that God was in me, there would be nothing that I could not know. This would be the test of faith that would follow me throughout my life.

My faith would become my shield against prejudice. I surrendered to the *"inner master and followed the light and sounds of the Universe"*. This was God manifesting Himself in me. This was not about religious affiliations. This was personal even before I was baptized. The Church saw fit to have me ordained as a deacon and later a trustee by the time I was twenty years old. I was thought to be wise beyond my years as the older members sought my council and the young looked up to me. This was an uncomfortable position for someone who was shy by nature and did not want to be seen. Also appointed to the deacon board was another young man, Willie Hughley, about my age. Willie and I would become valuable supporters of Reverend Stamps and the church. We remodeled the interior of the church, including installing new lighting, walls, and windows using skills I had learned from my dad. We were instrumental in helping to move the church from Tie Plant to a new location in the city of Louisville. It was decided that it was more economical to move the little church than to build a new one. So, the little church was loaded onto a flatbed truck and moved. Willie and I made the repairs and joined in the joyous homecoming of Massey Zion Baptist Church. We had finally left behind the odor of creosote and tar and launched a new beginning. The church has since moved to another location facing Greenwood Cemetery and has now rebuilt its edifice with brick and stone and has expanded its membership to over one thousand. Willie remains loyal to the church. He seeks me out each time I visit the city and reminisce about the old days. We will long remember the time during a watch meeting night when the affairs of the church were being reported and discussed by Reverend Stamps, who was also treasurer. Watch meeting was held on New Years Eve, where members could express their thanks for the good things that God had done for them during the year and to renew their faith. This was also the time when affairs of the church were discussed. This included a financial reporting and plans for the coming year. On this night Reverend Stamps was accused of stealing from the church. One of the original founding members and Deacon of the church demanded the pastor's resignation. The heated discussion almost became ugly when it was learned that the disgruntled deacon had a pistol in his possession. No proof of theft was ever found and the deacon did not leave the church. However, there were a few defections who found homes in other congregations.

    It was here I learned to understand and sing Negro Spirituals. I sang in the church choir, formed a trio with my sister, Leona, and another female church member and toured the city and near by towns. Leona and I knew all the gospel touring groups of the time-- The Spirit of Memphis, The Dixie Humming Birds, The Davis Sisters, The Caravans, The Soul Stirs featuring the legendary Sam Cooke, The Five Blind Boys of Mississippi, and many others. I remember when the Golden Gate Quartet came to town, Leona and I were too young to attend the concert alone that was being held in the segregated downtown concert hall. The Golden Gate Quartet and Mahalia Jackson were the most popular Negro gospel singers during this period that were followed and accepted by White audiences. My older sister, Lorene, took us to the concert. We had to enter through the back door of the concert hall and up the back stairs to the balcony. It did not matter for this brief moment I had witnessed an event that would never be repeated. A few years later I became the tenor for a quartet we named the Golden Tones. We became well known and attracted a large following where ever we went. Later a touring member and traveling companion of the famous Five Blind Boys of Alabama joined our group. Our reputation attracted interest from a recording company. However, for me it was time for college, so I decided to leave the group and close this phase of my life.

My sister, Leona, and I remained supportive to each other through most of our adult lives. She was married by age twenty. Our family was concerned at her decision at such a young age, since expectations for her were so high. She was an outstanding student with talents far beyond most of our generation. She married a man who had a good sense of humor that made her laugh. Perhaps, this was his most redeeming characteristic, yet we accepted her decision. He and his family were practicing Jehovah Witnesses. Soon after their marriage Leona accepted his religion. Leona and I remained close speaking to each other almost daily. This closeness would wane over the years as one might expect. I continued our family tradition of having Christmas celebrations at Mom's house and later at my sister, Lorene's, house. These events grew and were celebrated by family members throughout the country. They would all converge, some fifty to one hundred, to see what Baby Brother, the name I was always known by, had prepared for the celebration.

For weeks before Christmas I would carefully select a theme for the celebration, design and prepare menus, and spend days and hours preparing the meals. Coming home for Christmas was an event I would not miss no matter where I was or the circumstance of my employment. I went home! This ritual would continue for years, even though Jehovah Witnesses did not celebrate Christmas. No one questioned my efforts to bring the family together during this special time of the year and no one refused the gifts I shared. Leona and her family did not attend the festivities and I understood. One day my Mother announced that she had joined the Witnesses; later my sister, Lorene, had joined. However, the festivities continued at Lorene's house until 1999. Politely, I was informed by Lorene that the congregation had asked her to curtail the celebration. All of my life I had never missed a Christmas season with my family, now the party was over. This would be my test of faith. The Christmas season was not about the proof of the date of Christ's birth, but a celebration on His birth. Date, time, or season is not important. For me faith was not a test of ideology, but rather a personal declaration not to be argued or debated. "Exactness" could never be found in words. Now, I had lost the one person to whom no other could compare. Leona remains on a pedestal even though I can not observe her birthday, and to my deep chagrin the communication has ceased. I am left to try and understand what happened to the bond we shared and the trust we had in each other from the day of our birth. Perhaps, the baptismal we shared in the little church in Tie Plant did not have the same lasting meaning for her as it did for me, or her new found beliefs required total obedience to her spouse. I can still accept her decision, even though I must be seen as an un-repenting heathen and non believer. We do not see each other much anymore. I guess the stress is too great for both of us. God is still the God of the Universe.

Chapter 12

REFLECTIONS

Where we live or how we live is of little consequence.
What is important is to live.
    Ernest Dimnet, *What we live by*

To My Granddaughter, Katherine
Thelma Webb Wright

You can't imagine how wonderful it was to have you spend a day and night with me. I wish we lived closer so we could enjoy more visits. In contemplating your question of what I believe is important in life my mind always returns to one thought..."Be yourself in all situations".

That sounds easy, but in reflecting on my 81 years I realize there were times when I didn't know who "myself" was! After surviving numerous stupid and costly mistakes I have learned who "myself" is and what I need to do to be myself!

First... I must always be honest.

Second... before doing anything, I must try to project on how I will feel AFTER I do whatever it is. Then, I have to decide if I want to live with that feeling for the rest of my life or would I rather put myself in a position to avoid that feeling? Would I be doing whatever it is, to win approval of someone else, or would I be receiving my own approval?

Third... when I sense someone is trying to manipulate me, I may need to say "no" and perhaps say "no" without explanation, without being defensive, unkind or angry.

Fourth... I have learned to love, respect myself and laugh at myself. There is humor in any situation and that often gives a positive memory of what could have been an unhappy memory.

Five... it really doesn't matter what happens to us in life. What does matter is how we react to it. And how we react is our own choice.

Six...life is a gift; don't be afraid to live it. When you fall on your face, get up and move on. This is a great way to learn!

Seven... money is a necessity, but it should not be priority one for living. By some standards of judging I am poor. By my standard of judging I am wealthy. I don't have money in a bank. My wealth is in friends and family.

So my dear, be yourself in all ways that enables you to love, respect, enjoy life and have no regrets with yourself. Don't follow the crowd, follow your heart.

Development! Development!
Keith Severin

Yesterday was a good, but long day, different, for sure. We left home at 8AM, drove to the metro in Vienna, took it into Washington, DC and walked over to the Smithsonian National Museum of American History. It was a day-long seminar on "The Art Song- Music in Love with Poetry." Lots of good examples and sketches of interesting music, some recorded and some – the best – live. I guess from what I learned, art song is really poetry set to music, and Steven Blier – one of our friends and absolutely the best "musicologist" I know – said that music should help make the poetry understood better. After a full day there in the auditorium of The Hall of Musical Instruments in the Museum, we reversed our trip and got home at 6:15. Lots to think about – and those thoughts do go well beyond, far above the fortress like appearance Washington has taken on. Totally…

Eisenhower said we should be wary of the "industrial – military" complex. Today, we've got to look out for the "industrial – security" complex. So much going on under the guise of "security."

In days gone by, say 10-12-15 years ago – back when there were more deer than houses and roads around here – I would have had peas in the ground by now, planted them on George Washington's birthday weekend. Usually, the ground still had some frost in it, but I got the peas planted so they would be in the ground and ready to come up when the conditions got right. I suppose I could do that still, but there is so little place left for the deer, because of "development," that they figure it's easier to just come to our pea patch than browse where woods used to be. Yes, the deer eat strawberry plants right down to the ground too, and that really bothers Barbara. So, no more pea or strawberry patches, only "DEVELOPMENT!!"

We did enjoy Chicago. Say two operas – Fidelio and Tosca. One of our good friends, Alan Held, sang in Fidelio, and just by coincidence our son, Kenneth, was in Chicago where he had 48 hours "lab time" to use equipment at the Argonne National Laboratory. It worked out that Ken, who is also a good friend of Alan's, was able to get to the opera with us. After the opera, we went backstage and visited with Alan and then we all went to the Italian Village for what was a late dinner.

On Saturday afternoon Barbara and I went out to the Argonne Lab where Ken had it arranged – much security – to show us around, show us his work and also get an overall view of the place – huge and so very well put together. Lab time at Argonne is at a premium, able to obtain only after stringent requirements are met, and it is allotted on an hourly basis. Ken just takes it all in stride. He said there are 36 "work stations," (I call them) each able to do a different function.

Ken had received a copy of his book which had just been published in the Netherlands. "Energy Dispersive Spectra of Rock Forming Crystals," whatever that is. It looks quite impressive. The graphics and charts are something!!

Ken's time at Argonne was up on Monday, so was back to Fairbanks, Alaska the next day, at the university and his classes. Then, on Thursday he went to Eagle, on the Yukon River, and did the communications work at that checkpoint in the Yukon Quest, the 1,000 mile sleddog race he helps with every year. He was there several days for that, and reported he was glad to get home and get his own dogs harnessed and out for a run. Whew!!!

THE OLD IRON KETTLE
Harriet Burgess

In my family there exists an old iron kettle dating back to pre-Civil War days. It first appeared at the old homeplace called "Leeton" in Chantilly, VA. It was big, black, round and three-footed, hanging from an iron three-legged tripod.

In its early life it stood in the backyard at Leeton where the slaves made lye soap in it, which in turn was used to wash work clothes on the farm. It had many uses over the years until my grandmother acquired it.

When grandmother married and moved across the field to her new home she took the old kettle with her. During her years there on her farm she boiled work clothes in it to get out stubborn grease and dirt. Gradually the old kettle became a flower pot with a chip out of the top and a crack down the side.

As a child on her farm I remember once when the 'city cousins' had come out for a visit. We were all running and playing tag and Cousin George decided to take a short cut by attempting to jump over the kettle. His knee hit the chipped edge and split his skin to the kneecap bone. He carries that scar to this day.

The Old Iron Kettle

When my husband and I built our home across two fields from Leeton, I acquired the old kettle and continued using it as a flower pot, planted with lots of petunias as the seasons rolled by.

Today the old iron kettle is still a flower pot with petunias cascading down its sides, only now it resides in Fauquier County in the front yard of my second home. I'm sure it will be passed on to the next generation at some future time.

WORLD WAR 11 REFLECTIONS
Harriet Burgess

I completed my grade school years while living with my maternal grandparents on their farm in Chantilly, Virginia. In 1938 I went to live with my mother and new stepfather in Arlington, Virginia in an apartment. There I attended Thomas Jefferson Jr. High School and later Washington-Lee High School. The change from farm life to apartment dwelling was mind-boggling and I was not a 'happy camper'.

During World II a girl friend and I planted a "Victory Garden" in a vacant field, supplied by Arlington County and located four blocks from our apartments. We tended it faithfully, raising vegetables and flowers. My farm years experience came in handy for this project. We enjoyed many of the bounties from this garden and felt we were doing our part for the war effort.

I had three uncles in the service at this time and many anxious moments were spent worrying over their safety and eagerly reading their V-Mail letters from the European front and the South Pacific. V-Mail letters sent from home to overseas were written on thin paper, folded and sealed all in one self contained unit. The soldier's letters home were also sent V-Mail but were censored and microfilmed for military violations. Mention of maneuvers, size of military units, or battle plans were blanked out of their letters by the military censors before being sent home. All of my uncles came home safely in 1945 when the war ended.

One uncle had malaria off and on the rest of his life as a result of jungle fighting in the South Pacific. Another uncle received the Purple Heart for an injury sustained to his hand while in France. My third uncle, who had joined the Merchant Marines, caught pneumonia while off the coast of England and was sent back to the United States to recuperate in a hospital in Sheepshead Bay, New York. This was a year before the war ended. He was finally sent back to the farm and designated essential to the war effort. He was also greatly needed by his now widowed mother in operating the farm.

Uncle Bill McWhorter served with Gen. Patton's Army in Europe, WWII

Uncle George McWhorter served in Army, South Pacific, WWII

Uncle Sam McWhorter joined the Merchant Marine and went to England, WWII

There were many hardships to endure during the war but we willingly put up with them. Automobiles were no longer manufactured for the consumer—the factories had converted to turning out military vehicles. Ration books were issued for many items such as sugar, meats, dairy products, shoes, etc. I remember the difficulty with the substitute for butter. It was produced in a plain white 1 pound block that looked like lard and came with a little capsule of liquid orange coloring. To obtain the look of butter the capsule contents were squirted into the lard-like mass and worked back and forth until the coloring was evenly distributed. The end result was called oleomargarine, named for the oleo oil extracted from animal fats.

Silk stockings were non-existent. The silk was used to make parachutes for the military. Women substituted rayon stockings that produced a streaked effect and definitely didn't have 'that sheer look'. Leg makeup was also used to give a tanned look in place of stockings. It had to be carefully applied to the legs to avoid streaking. Occasionally a store was rumored to have gotten in a small shipment of silk stockings and a line would immediately form for several blocks—usually to no avail. Gas coupons were issued to the public and non-essential users were issued 'A stickers'. If the monthly allotment was used up early, you did without! My grandparents on the farm were entitled to a larger allotment of gas as operation of farm machinery was essential.—even then there was never enough. In the early days of the war two of my uncles drove taxicabs in Washington, D.C. Cabs were considered essential also and more gas was available for their use. Often left over coupons were given to my grandparents for farm use.

Discarded farm machinery and pieces of junk metal were collected by local farmers and contributed to the war effort for conversion to war machines. All over the country 'scrap drives' were organized by the Boy and Girl Scouts and other civic organizations. Contests were held to see who could collect the most in a community. Parts for repairing broken down farm machinery were scarce and even impossible to get in some instances. Improvising and often the use of old baling wire from the used up hay bales were put to good use in many cases.

Our ears were always tuned to the radio for the latest war news. Well known reporters of that time were Eric Seviereid, Walter Cronkite and Edward R Murrow, who reported from London during the 'blitz'. The 'blitz' was a heavy concentration of bombs dropped on London by the Germans for long periods of time. This was a time of fear and anxiety for all on the home front. The Army had journalists traveling with some of their units, reporting on the battles. Ernie Pyle, noted for his human portrayals, endeared himself to the GIs, writing many humorous and personal stories from the front lines. Eventually he lost his life in a jeep accident while reporting.

When D-Day finally arrived, the country wildly celebrated. Germany surrendered in May 1945. Thousands gathered on Pennsylvania Avenue in

Washington, D.C. in front of the White House, where they danced and cheered in the street with the returning soldiers and sailors. Joyful families joined the mad jubilation.

In September 1945 the war ended in the South Pacific (V-J Day) with the surrender of Japan, and the country was at peace again—ticker tape parades down Broadway in New York City and celebrations all across America.

Upon graduation from high school I attended George Washington University in Washington, D.C. for two years and worked briefly for the United Nations Relief & Rehabilitation Agency (UNNRA)—who provided relief to foreign countries devastated by the war.

There were few men at social events during the war, most were serving their country. The men still out of uniform were looked down upon—regarded as 'draft dodgers' (excuses to stay out of the service), or '4fers' (a term used for those who did not meet medical qualifications for the service). When I entered the government, there were still some service organizations operating. The USO (United Serviceman's Organization) entertained at military installations and canteens throughout the country as well as overseas.

I joined a group of government girls who were bused once a week to Ft. Belvoir, Virginia, (an Army post), where we danced and visited with the soldiers at the canteen. These dances were quite popular with the servicemen who were still in the Army and many lasting friendships were made, even some marriages.

The world was settling down once again as we entered the postwar years.

My Dad
Eugene Tucker

There were times when I could feel the anxiety and frustration in my parents during those early years. Upon reflection it seemed as though we had all been trapped in an endless whirlpool of strife and denial as we searched for inner peace, food and shelter. Money was our primary source of irritation, for my father was not able to earn enough to feed and house his family. This frustration was to haunt him in some fashion for the remainder of his life even though he never murmured a single word of despair. He did not need to utter a word, for his persona would tell the story of a man deeply troubled by his fate. Here in a little town in a little house nestled beside the railroad tracks that lead north to Chicago, Illinois and south to the Gulf of Mexico the family sought to hold on to life. This was Grenada, Mississippi in the late 1930's.

Tie Plant was some four to six miles south of our house. Each morning my father would rise at four or five AM and make the long walk down the railroad tracks to Tie Plant where he would spend long hours either carrying cross ties or working on the cranes. Mom had packed his lunch in a tin molasses bucket, stuffed with biscuits, fat back, rice and greens. He liked banana pudding sandwiches, which Mom hated to make. To a small boy the accounts of his father's exploits and expressions of his physical prowess were all rewarding and I would spend many hours wishing my father would tell me more stories. It was not until later that I learned that for those long hours of hardship and work my father received one dollar and fifty cents on a good week. Like many men in our little community my father would seek refuge in drink and gambling and on some occasion the rewards of his labor never reached the anxious hands of our mother. Sadden by his dilemma my father would stay away from home for two or three days rather than face the wanting eyes of his family. A similar plight was shared by most of our neighbors.

On occasion the women would meet after long hours of working in the fields or in the kitchens of their "white folks" and talk about their shiftless husbands or about "Two Bit Sue" who spent her evenings raising money for her daily bread by selling physical pleasures in and around the train station. With a little boy's inquisitiveness about the exploits of loose women, I would strain to hear every detail without letting it be known that I was listening. Oh! It was so much fun to be a boy of five and share the joys and intimate secrets of grown-ups. Maybe they knew about me and all the other little boys like me, but privacy in that little community was not part of the local philosophy. It had never been and it probably would never come.

About every woman I knew or heard about went to work everyday. Domestic work was by far the most popular. When things really got tough Mom had to take in washing and ironing or go into White people's houses for whatever work she could get. A days work would sometimes net fifty cents for which Mom would give back in exchange for a piece of meat or other items of food for her family. Old clothes and shoes were of particular value. Many of those White people were kind and gentle even though they insisted that all Negroes come to the back door and address them as "mister" or "miss". Racial superiority had completely engulfed this town. Even White children had to be addressed as mister or miss by their nannies or any other Negro person whether old or as young as I. Whenever there was a White person on the sidewalk, Negroes knew without being told that they must get off the street to allow a White person to pass, even if it meant walking in the street and avoiding oncoming cars. Everyone seemed to know his or her place. Negroes knew the consequences of stepping out of line. In a little store where we would go to buy candy and chewing gum or a little grocery we were fortunate to buy, a mongoloid White boy roamed around the store to frighten the little Black children who came to spend their pennies. You could buy a quarter stick of butter. The store was willing to take whatever money you had in exchange for something of equivalent value. On reflection it is strange that we even had any pennies, but, then too, we would run errands for those Negroes who had booming bootleg operations. Children were often called upon to make a delivery because the sheriff never suspected us or perhaps we were not worth worrying about.

These deprived and destitute Negroes were very inventive and discovered many ways of making ends meet. White people were the source of income from trades like sewing, tending lawns, washing windows, and even prostitution. On one occasion one prostitute who had sold her pleasures to many prominent White men about town was killed by a group of irate wives. These women had discovered their husbands' playmate and resolved the matter by abducting the prostitute and taking her near the fairgrounds and stabbed her with ice picks until she was dead. As was the case in this town and in most other towns in the south nothing was done about atrocities like this. A public menace had been given her just reward. And once again an example of white supremacy was displayed before the Negroes in this community. "The price of sin is surely death," was a typical theme from the pulpit of the churches on Sunday morning. If you do wrong God will find you out. And again the story was closed and life returned to normal until the next result of sin would provoke our awareness of man's inhumanity to man.

White people were not the only source of income for Negroes. Home brew may have been even more rewarding. It required a great deal of resourcefulness, for prohibition was the law of the land and to be caught could mean a stay in the horrible jail where a "Nigger hating" sheriff rode heard. He was known to take Niggers from their cells for his amusement. Some never returned. It was known that the Sheriff had pinned a murder charge on two black youths who were returning home from Church one Sunday night. As the story goes the Sheriff had a long disagreement with another White man who lived near the town. On this night the Sheriff developed his sinister plot to eliminate his old nemesis once and for all. The venom and cowardice engulfed this vindictive enforcer of law and order in this little town. Like a thief in the night he lurked in the darkness waiting for the opportunity to fire the shot that would kill his long time foe and eventually destroy an innocent Negro family. The shot that rang out that night and the events that followed were typical testimony on the lips of Negro people recounting events in their lives and the lives of their friends. As the story continued two brothers were returning home from night services at a near by church. They had traveled this long dusty road many times playing and frolicking as young men do, carefree and happy to be alive. This night the joy would end forever, for hidden behind a clomp of bushes lurked the feared Sheriff with the blood of his foe still warm on his hands and with a sinister plot developed in his mind. Just as he had stolen the life of his old adversary the Sheriff stepped from behind the bushes as the boys passed and ordered the boys to halt or be killed. The reputation of this Sheriff was well known to these young men and the urge to run was quickly quelled at the thought of a sure death. They stopped in their tracks. The Sheriff informed them that he was taking them into custody for murder. The weight of being Black was suddenly upon them. They along with their family were threatened with murder if they revealed the fact that the Sheriff had forced his will upon them. The trial revealed no evidence that the boys were guilty of any crime. There was never a motive established; no weapon found; and only the Sheriff's word was considered. The trial was held after a long wait in jail during which time both boys were fed sparingly. As expected they were found guilty. One was sentenced to death on the gallows. The other boy would be sentenced to life in prison.

My uncle Gene was in jail at the time for an assault on another Negro man. My uncle watched the case unfold and was ordered along with other inmates to witness the end. When the day of the supreme power of the law was to be exerted, the boy was too thin for his body to dislodge his life. The gallows were in place and the executioners were in waiting to again show the power of "justice." The early morning hours when all are asleep does the keeper of "justice" creep. This was a sight that stayed with my uncle through World War 1, where he was awarded the Purple Heart for Valor and for the remainder of his life. Jail inmates were required to watch the proceeding so that they could see what would happen to them if any one of them committed a crime, or was suspected of committing a crime, or caught in the vicinity of a crime committed against a White person. They gathered at the windows of their cells in full view of the gallows that had been erected a few days before. It was not long before the hanging party had gathered all drunk and fortified for the job they were about to do. The young man to die was called out. He was marched to the gallows and permitted to say his last words, *"God in Heaven, you know that I did not kill Mr. Crenshaw."* A one hundred pound sack of sand was attached to his waist because the events that had transpired since that night on the long dusty road had left him holding barely to life with nothing more than skin and bones to show that he was still alive. He adorned the steps of the gallows with only the hope that God would receive his soul and pardon him for his sins and for those who were about to take his life. The black cap of death was put in place and then the noose. All were in waiting for the final order. It came but the agony and the struggle for life was not over for some minutes, not before his high-topped shoes had been kicked free from his feet. Then, there was the silence and pronouncement of death by the doctor and the clergy.

The remaining brother was to linger only a short time in jail. It was believed that he was fed poison until death claimed him. His mother and sister all died unexplained deaths. With one shot and a pull of a trigger an entire family had been destroyed. The White man's power had once again been put on exhibit in the Negro community. Recounting this story to a young boy by his parents does wonders for the image of the White man. It assures that fear of him will reach down even to the "littlest angel." Many stories and accounts of the White man's deeds were told in the little shanties at night. In many cases these stories resulted in the children's education in preparation for their life's work in the fields and on the railroads. There would be little chance for formal learning. Dad found the courage in the 1940's to board the train headed north in search of a better life for himself and his family.

For thirty years this man who wore a floppy hat, dipped snuff, wore baggy pants and brogan shoes, and suffered from severe asthma answered the call for work each and every day of his life. Even when he was obviously sick the urge to work propelled him towards the bus stop at 38th and Broadway in Louisville, Kentucky. One day he could go no more. I was summoned home for Dad had been diagnosed with a blood clot on the brain. I would become the head of the family and continue to show him the love that he had shown me. Medical science was not advanced enough at the time to risk his life through an operation. So, we would have to witness his decay day by day for several years, before he would be rescued from his bondage of life before the age of sixty five. He was dressed and lay in state in the Funeral Parlor on Broadway Street. As I gazed upon his face and examined his weather beaten hands these words came to me:

"The lifeless remains of my father lie before us today. The shock of his death will not be heard around the world, for he was not a famous man, nor a statesman. He had done nothing that the world considered important. However, his life was as precious and priceless as any creation of God, so we are here to witness the final episode in the life and time of Eugene Tucker, Sr., just another grain of sand in God's creation.

He was born on March 8, 1905, in a place too small to be placed on a map. He remembered it as Big Black, Mississippi, a swamp which was inhabited by wild hogs, bears, wolves and panthers. His early years were trying ones, for his father died before his sixth birthday. He became accustomed to work soon after he ran away from home before his seventh birthday to avoid the wrath of a stepfather. The remainder of his life was all work and hardship. His only son who proudly bears his name must now carry the torch."

My Love of Books
Helen P. Hannett

My parents gave me a great love for books. It started before I was two years old, and Mom would place many beautiful golden books around me on the back patio with sunlight streaming down on them. Any little child would notice the bright pastel books and interesting artwork on the cover and figure that they might be really interesting. One book, printed in the 1940's, was a cozy little story about a baby and his house. In the 1970's I decorated by baby's room to resemble the one from the book, including appliquéing beautiful calico and gingham flowers on the homemade white café curtains. I had not seen the book since the '40's, but it had been imprinted on my heart.

In 1950 when I was almost three, we first moved onto the army post in Texas, my father would spend a lot of time reading bedtime stories to me. He read *Little Sally Mandy Stories, Brer Rabbit, Aesop's Fables* and all of the regular fairy tales that children love. After reading each of Aesop's stories and each fairy tale, he would ask me what lesson I had learned from that story. He would warmly affirm whether I told him. The benefit of the morals and lesson learned from Daddy's story hour was that we understood the lessons because of hearing the stories. We gained wisdom.

Daddy stopped reading to us when he couldn't find certain Dickens' Christmas stories that he wanted to read. I think he thought there were some by Dickens written specially for children. *A Christmas Carol* was not the one. "There was another," he said. How I missed his reading to us then.

One day we had an interesting surprise when the Compton's Picture Encyclopedia salesman visited our house on post. Prior to this my father had decided to buy an encyclopedia. The salesman showed sample books which Mother looked at while my brother and I climbed onto her lap or surrounded her chair to see, also.

My parents bought the set that I secretly loved. It was a 1949 edition covered in black leather with an overall intaglio design of flowers, leaves, hearts, diamond shapes and rectangles and was especially attractive to children. The inside cover was filled with dreamy colored pictures. In fact, my mother's nickname for me was "Dreamy". I didn't know what a knight was; neither could I name the Taj Mahal, the Chinese junk the igloo, pyramid or a city of the future pictured there among the billowing blue clouds. My heart was captured by the pictures. Looking at the silver knight in armor, lance drawn, on horseback in grey fog, I felt like I was beginning a mystical journey with my life of books.

Everyday Mom read to my brother, Mike, and me from the new encyclopedia complete with colored pictures. One of my favorites was "Adventures of Blackie and Ginger, The Story of two Little Bears." Another was "What Sinbad Found Out in the Desert, The Story of a Young Camel". Many of the volumes featured fictional stories of baby animals like these and gave us so much delight and enjoyment. A few years later, holding our new baby sister in her lap, Mom even played some of the finger games with little songs that we learned from another volume. We all knew how to make my little sister laugh with these songs.

On vacation Dad heard me read some of my baby sister's little cloth books on the alphabet. I could read bat, cat mat, can, man, and fan from that cloth book because I learned from him. He was pleased.

My parents brought me for an interview with the principal at Incarnate Word Grade School in San Antonio. It was a new white brick and marble school built in time for the post-World War II baby boom. It was a Catholic private girl's boarding and day school, across from a buffalo reservation. There was a high school on the second level, a college down the street, a convent with infirmary for aged nuns and novitiate for student nuns. I was accepted as a first grade day hop for the fall. After the interview I came home and sat on the back step. In my hands I held the student handbook upside down and tried excitedly to read it. I still remember how it looked upside down more than fifty years later.

I had to take a city bus which picked up the kids on the army post a couple of blocks down the street. I was the only one on the post going to that school besides a kind "Grace Kelly" look alike high school girl, who baby sat us later and taught Mike and me to dance the waltz.

The best thing about Incarnate Word was the wonderful books on the shelves in each classroom. The books were graded Dick and Jane types with fathers and mothers and brothers and sisters and babies and pets featured, subjects that every first grader experienced or wanted. They spoke to the heart and were universally good. Before the invention of "political correctness", the writers of the stories had poured the souls and grace of real characters into the writings so that the young readers' lives were greatly sweetened with comfort and joy. Readers also learned how to lead good lives whether rich or poor. I could never get enough of these stories of happy homes.

At the end of my first day I was able to read a whole small pre-primer. I'll never forget that or the good feeling it gave me.

The way Sister Mary Eileen and later Sister Charles Joseph taught us to read was first, going over and over the alphabet till everyone knew it. She taught us all the sounds of the vowels and the consonants, but also how they felt and looked like when sounded. That was the clincher for owning the ability to read them. There were vowel combinations of which we had to learn all the possible sounds for each. Everyday we drilled. There were rhythms and patterns that sounded like "rap" poems. We recited all the possible sounds of the vowel "A" and then respectively for "E," "I," "O," "U." The methods today that most resemble the way we were taught to read are the Lindamond Bell Method and the Phono-Graphix Method combined.

In the second grade one of the most important things in my life happened. I had Sister Charles Joseph Cushen for my teacher. This is how I first came to her attention. One of the second grade girls handed Sister back a brown bag with Sister's broken alarm clock inside, saying that her "father couldn't fix it."

"Does anybody else here have a father who likes to fix things? I will have trouble getting up without an alarm clock."

"Who thinks their father might be able to fix my alarm clock?"

Since my hand was up, I received the brown bag with my teacher's clock which I carried along with my book bag out to the bus stop. Accidentally, I dropped the bag, and when I looked inside, I found that the glass was totally smashed into pieces. Although I was very scared when I got home, I handed Mom the bag and said, "Sister Charles Joseph wanted to know if Dad could fix her alarm clock." When I returned to school, I was carrying what I suspect was a brand new identical alarm clock. In later years when Mom was in her 80's, I asked her about that broken clock which Sister entrusted to me for Daddy to fix. Did she know that I was the last girl in the class to volunteer? Did she guess that I had dropped it, and how I still was stunned that she and Dad had simply replaced it". Mom just gave me the most beautiful smile that I will never forget when I told her how happy I was to give my teacher back that new clock, and said thank you!

The nuns worked for no pay back then. But, that kind deed of my parents somehow won me Sister Charles Joseph's studied interest. From that moment on, through second grade and then through third grade, as she was promoted along with our class, she would not let any bad behavior on my part or that of classmates go uncorrected. She frequently gave up one of her two recesses daily to help me work on my penmanship and my reading.

Sister Charles Joseph's used the most beautiful Palmer Method handwriting herself. It was classically beautiful in her letter foundation, and she expected ours to be similar with a great deal of supervised practice. But, she intrigued all of us the most by her use of peacock blue ink. She had us buy fountain pens and bottles of ink, and we all wanted peacock blue ink just like her. To this day on my vanity is a bright blue kin well and a smooth pen. In the eight grade, my father would give me a beautiful gold and red fountain pen with rhinestones because I loved to write letters.

Sister Charles Joseph intensified all the reading drills that we did in first grade and also worked on spelling and cursive handwriting. In addition, she had to prepare our second grade class for our First Holy Communion. That meant she had to make sure our entire class memorized and understood the catechism and learned all our prayers. We practiced penmanship by copying beautiful children's prayers that she brought with her from her native Ireland. The result of all this work and repetition on our part as students was not only knowledge of the faith but an ability to read and a friend and a pen pal for life.

A penmanship session

One day I was at home after school in my upstairs room that faced our front street, and I saw a recently new classmate carrying a large book under her arm and walking alongside her mother. Even though they were far away from my window, I could definitely read the title on that large book—*Peter Rabbit*. I realized they were walking to the library. It was from that moment that I felt an intense longing and passion for a library card, and to this day I still think of that book under Rosemary's arm. I had asked Mom if I could get a card, but she said with my little sister the books would get lost or torn. I just had to make do with the books at school and the storybooks that we bought.

In one of my school books was a story about a girl who owned three beautiful dolls. Nothing was as luxurious or wonderful as owning three dolls. With three dolls you had multiple characters for doll playing dramas. Well, when I finished third grade, we left for Daddy's new post in Oahu, Hawaii. Once there my deepest wish came true. It started then while crossing the ocean on board our ship the *Ainsworth*, the fire alarm had sounded when my parents were attending a party. When they returned to our room, they were surprised to see that I had used a ladder to get the lifejackets down for my brother, sister and myself. We were all suited up and about to walk out to the lifeboats following the captain's instructions. We didn't know it was only a fire drill and not for real. But, from that moment, my parents looked upon me as not a child anymore but both capable and responsible. Once in our now home and new school, I registered at three different libraries and had three different library cards. At the Mt. Michael's School library the librarian, who was a new friend, would always hand me the latest new book on a saint's life. The second library that our class walked to with our teacher had books that young girls would love like *The Old Fashioned Doll, Hans Brinker and the Silver Skates,* and all of Laura Ingalls Wilder's books and those of Louisa May Alcott. With the third card I got at the post library, I took out an entire Twin international series of graded fiction about the adventures of twin girls written by Lucy Fitch Perkins. I also found many biographies of scientists like Madam Curie, Louis Pasteur, and of nurses like Clara Barton and Florence Nightingale. I also took out all the fairy tales from foreign countries both folktales and those of Grimm and Anderson. So you see, for me the growing was in the journey, and Hawaii was like a paradise for me because of the abundance of fabulous library books. Many of these I was never able to find again. But, those library cards started me on the kind of life I treasure and helped me find many friends who have also shared with me a real love of good stories both in and out of books. And now, here I am, even trying to write one for you.

Chapter 13

WORDS OF WISDOM

Tell me what company thou keepest, and I'll tell thee what thou art.
                                              Cervantes, *Don Quixote*

Now, Hear This
Eugene Tucker

Education

Learning is a humbling experience. The more you think you know; the more you realize how little you know.

Politics

Questioning accepted norms can be perilous. Socrates lost his life for questioning the government in his native Greece. He drank his potion, died, and gave the world the age of reason. Then there was Mendelssohn and his concepts on genetics. This conflict with the church lead to his death. Copernicus would fair little better with his theory about the earth revolving around the sun. In our generation we have witnessed the struggles for the right to vote, women's suffrage, civil rights for minorities, the right to die, the definition of life, and the meaning of marriage and family. Each and every day we watch our leaders defining and redefining themselves at the expense of others as they struggle with the rhetoric of the day. Their rhetoric divides a nation and the world with certain destructive consequences. Yet they continue to talk about world peace and unity at home. Perhaps, it is time to rethink the meaning of "politician" and the "party line". Politicians bring wars, promote promiscuity, liberate children, divide families, and seek power to control every aspect of our lives all in the name of leadership. They use the laws they make to become rich and then bash the rich to incite the poor. Little wonder that "ordinary people" are courted each election season, because politicians are not ordinary. Perhaps we know too much about them to cast our vote. Does it sound strange that electability is measured by the amount of money spent per voter? One without wealth or a major war chest or the ability to incite the poor may never become president.

Science, Technology, and Man

Are all men born equal? This question begs discussion as we grapple with cloning, stem cells, artificial insemination, surrogate motherhood, sperm banks, intravenous fertilization, and genetic research. We can now create life and give it our own traits and characteristics. We are ready to control the size and nature of the species, both human and animal, and to propagate them throughout the universe as we now know it. One day we may announce that we have been to the outer edge of the universe and have not found God. The biblical creation theory will be brought into serious question and replaced with scientific proof. Texts will be rewritten and old dogmas placed on shelves to show the evolution of man. For those holding on to their "God" theory they would be encouraged by clerics to keep this safety net in place as they struggle to survive the onslaught of science and technology. Man as we know him today is likely to be quite different. Who's to say that the male portion of "Man" may become extinct or reduced in significance as technology changes the manner in which the specie is reproduced?

Democracy and the Social Order

Here we are in the 21st century again facing a world at odds with itself. Many of us remember the jubilation of the "civilized world" following the end of the world wars and the fall of the Berlin Wall. Some of us have read about the hundred years' war, the fall of the Roman Empire, and all of the recorded struggles of man trying to define himself, his society, and establish norms for his existence within his own established environment. It soon became evident that his very existence also depended on his neighbors with whom he interacted for commerce and even a sense of security. As man became more and more entrenched in his own ideology clashes within and without his confines became an expected way of life. Today, after thousands of years of history-- oral, written, and discovered, there appears to be little we have learned about the nature of man. Yes, we are all different and view the world through our own circumstance and resist when the world tries to look in on us.

Man's quest for riches and status resulted in the establishment of a democracy in the Americas. The struggle for power and world dominance began as those countries with means sought their piece of the prize. Time and civilization have not healed the rift between nations as their leaders flex their muscles and escalate their rhetoric on the world stage, while charging their constituents to honor nationalism. Once there were statesmen who championed the cause of human existence; today they seem not to exist. Scholarly dialogue has given way to caustic recriminations, skepticism, and "gotcha". After all this is Democracy in America practiced for the world to see. Everyone among us seems to have all the answers, while no one seems willing to entertain the questions. Is this the price we pay for "freedom" and "liberty"? Or, are we witnessing the emergence of a new world order where chaos and turmoil will precede a new social order that will bring harmony among men of all nations? As my generation returns to the dust I trust that civilization as we know it has not run its course.

BIOGRAPHICAL SKETCHES

Eugene Tucker (Gene) lives with his wife and their six year old in Catlett, VA. Gene, a descendant of slaves, a former university professor, mathematician, and consultant, enjoys art collecting and discussing socio-political issues. He is intensely competitive having majored in math, physics, history, and the humanities. The family moved to Fauquier County Virginia in 1996, where he owns and manages a conference center.

Thelma Webb Wright, a passionate writer, lover of life, and your typical Gypsy, lives in Marshall, VA with designs on Florida. Thelma insists on being referred to as a senior, not elderly. Thelma and her family have lived in many parts of the country during her wonderful and enriched life. Thelma has successfully published *"Grandma, You're Lopsided!"* and *"Tramp Artist"*. She is a wonderful teacher and motivator with a strong will.

Harriet Burgess, born and raised in the Washington, DC metropolitan area with a family connection to the Civil War and its aftermath, she now lives in Marshall, VA and close to her children and grandchildren. Her passion is traveling and enjoying this vast and beautiful country. A trip a week is her motto, but she took precious time off to write some wonderful stories about her enriched life.

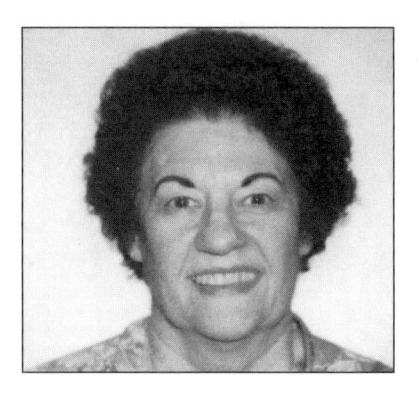

Keith Severin, if you ever heard of the Grapes of Wrath, meet him. Keith is the American Dream in the flesh. From abject poverty to earning a graduate degree from Stanford University with emphasis on agriculture and animal husbandry, and serving our country around the world from Samoa to Siberia is testament to courage and determination. Keith now lives near Warrenton, VA with his first love and wife who has shared his wonderful journey. Keith's passion for animals and agriculture continues with him today as he travels around the country admiring and judging many of man's best friends.

Helen Hannett, daughter of a military doctor who survived a bloody death march in WWII and POW camps, is a loving mother and homemaker. Helen is a lover of the classics, art, music and theatre. She enjoys the piano almost as much as she enjoys old books. Helen now lives in Warrenton, VA with her husband and seven children, whom she monitors with compassion.